Lauren

With love

Jack

The Little Things

www.mascotbooks.com

The Little Things: A Memoir of Paralysis, Motivation, and Pursuing a Meaningful Life

For more information, please contact:
Mascot Books
620 Herndon Parkway, Suite 320
Herndon, VA 20170
info@mascotbooks.com

Library of Congress Control Number: 2021910947

CPSIA Code: PRV0921A
ISBN-13: 978-1-64543-313-2

Printed in the United States

To my family.

THE LITTLE
THINGS

A MEMOIR OF PARALYSIS, MOTIVATION, AND PURSUING A MEANINGFUL LIFE

Jack Trottier
with Jason Anthony

CONTENTS

1

JANUARY 16, 2013

Stillness. Stillness and cold and calm. Snow blankets the trees and the yards and the roads. There is no sound.

Nothing moves. Only snowflakes falling from a gray sky onto my face. I don't try to brush them away. Each flake that lands on my cheeks is telling me to go to sleep. Everything is in slow motion. My eyes are closing; my lids are heavy. My hands tingle, and a weird, warm vibration pulses through my body, but there's something so comforting about lying in the snow in complete silence. I am drifting away.

Words cannot describe this calmness I feel.

"Jack, breathe. Breathe, Jack."

That's Paul. He is kneeling next to me, and in the distance is Eric. The three of us have the whole world to ourselves. But mostly I'm in my own world now, all alone. A world smothered in snow and closed off from the noise of real life.

Here's something I think about a lot. *I* did this. To myself. I built my own death trap.

I took my life into my own hands. Which, when you think about it, seems like a good thing, right? My life *should* be in my own hands.

We make choices all day long, mostly without thinking. Do what? Go where? With whom? When? Some decisions bother us all day long or keep us up at night as we think about pros and cons, risks and rewards. Are we more afraid of doing something or of not doing something? Do we want to do it, or do we just want to have done it? Is it "good" or "bad" or, most likely, somewhere in between?

Some of my decisions leaned more toward risk than safety, but not a lot. I was more into meeting a challenge than getting a hit of adrenaline. I was careful and bold at the same time.

I was a kid in motion, an athlete. Like everyone else, I liked to make my own decisions and choose my own adventures. I still do. The question, I guess, is how hard to push.

Odds are that nearly every decision we make, good or bad, will work out fine. Human population is increasing despite being full of adults who made the same bad decisions they warn kids about.

We all want to have fun but not if it means winning a Darwin award. We're scared to die, so we push the idea of death away and imagine a long, sweet life for ourselves.

I worked hard to make good things happen. On some days I was the quarterback who made the last-minute fourth quarter touchdown pass or the student who stayed up all night finishing his anatomy labs, and on other days I was that kid who saw a hill and a pile of snow as a blank canvas and thought, *Let's do this crazy thing.*

And so, on an otherwise ordinary day, I built my own death trap.

Except I'm not dying. Well, no more than you are. I'm really, really alive. I always have been. From day one I was that kid rolling, laughing, standing, running, throwing, jumping, living. I'm sitting here writing this with the same love for life that I've always had. The fact that I'm sitting down because I can't stand up doesn't change the equation, though there have been plenty of days when I thought it did. I'm still rolling along, even if the set of wheels beneath my ass isn't what I hoped for at age seventeen.

And so, on the day my story begins, as the snow came down, I took my life into my own hands. I got busy building my own death trap. I set it up and I packed it down. Then I geared up and launched myself into midair.

═══════════════════

Floating down into darkness. That's what it feels like, lying half-conscious in the snow. Like falling without the gravity. Or like all the weight in my body is being slowly, gently drained out of me into the snow.

It's that delicious sleep-is-happening feeling, but with a twist: I should be in pain. I should be sitting up, getting up, shaking it off. I should not be sinking deeper and deeper into a whiteout of the mind. I know that, but it's happening anyway. A few minutes ago, I was up with the snowflakes, and then I hit the ground. Now I'm floating somewhere in between.

What's better than a snow day? A snow day in high school. We're not just kids who stay home and play; we're kids who can jump in a car and play wherever we want. I was one of the first in my class to earn my license, and for nine months I'd been driving my friends around our little northern Massachusetts town in my old black Ford Explorer.

That's one of the things I miss the most. What's more real than that kind of freedom?

Well, pain is more real, actually. And so is fear. But I'm getting to that.

The snow wasn't doing much at five thirty a.m. when I learned that school was cancelled. A big January storm was about to hit us. I celebrated first by crawling back into bed for three hours and then by driving the Explorer through a few inches of snow to my friend Justin's place for a session of *NHL 12*.

But when Eric called, I hit the road again. The snow was coming down hard. Back at my house I grabbed my snowboarding gear and all the wood and plywood scraps I could scavenge from my mom's shed. Two minutes later I was at Eric's, having picked up our buddy Paul as he trudged down the middle of the snowy road.

Our "terrain park" was a bunch of junky lumber on a fifty-foot hill behind Eric's house. We called it The Wasteland. The wood scraps weren't ideal, but we were motivated. We shoveled and packed snow around the features we dreamed up, walked up to the shed at the top of Eric's hill, stepped into our snowboards, and launched.

Each day we got a little better, pulled off some new trick.

Building jumps is easy. Have shovel, will travel. All you need is a strong back and a weak mind. Shape it up and pack it down. The narrow and wide features we call rails and boxes require more precision, though. They need to be built rock solid so you can hit them hard from different angles. So we fixed up the sloppy stuff and improvised lines through the features, pushing ourselves to change it up and have fun.

That's the great thing about a terrain park. It's not about being the fastest snowboarder or the world's best rail or jump guy. It's about testing yourself against the physical puzzles that come rushing at you. It's about overcoming obstacles and trying to show off a bit when you can.

My dad, after hearing in the morning that my plan was to "just chill," had suggested I do something useful and go either to the gym or Nashoba. Later, my mother called to also suggest I go to Nashoba for the day. Nashoba Valley Ski Area is the small ski hill in Westford, Massachusetts, where I learned to snowboard and where my sister and I worked teaching new riders. Mom didn't like the sketchy scene at Eric's. She'd rather have me drive half an hour through the snowstorm to Nashoba than drive the two miles to The Wasteland.

But I loved making my own park. No lines, no crowds, just our own little world to build up, tear down, and rebuild. On somebody else's mountain, you're paying to be entertained. But when you make your own hill, even if it's tiny, you create your own entertainment. Eric was even more obsessed, always outside fixing some feature or building a new jump. Neither one of us had the best body type for doing tricks; you want to be short and compact, and Eric was even taller and rangier than me. It didn't matter, though. Every day at school we talked about our next trick.

Despite my parents' concerns, it felt like a good day to go riding at Eric's. What better way to spend a snow day than strapped to a board in my own little world?

I first hit the snow when I was four years old. My sister, Sam, had done the same. And it was Mom that put us there. She was a ski instructor at Nashoba for over ten years, and we followed in her tracks. But long before I started to teach at Nashoba I'd made the switch to riding a board instead of skis and gotten into tricks and big air.

It started when I was in second grade. My family took a ski vacation at Steamboat Springs, Colorado, and that's where I first saw the scary amazing circus that is a terrain park, with its rails, jumps, and massive half-pipe. I knew right away it was a circus I could join, because I saw some local ten-year-old catch air on a fifty-footer and disappear downslope.

By fifth grade, the year my parents divorced, I'd switched from sticks to a board and become as obsessed with it as I was with football. Maybe I wasn't exactly Olympic material, but by sixteen I had competed in a few big-air and slopestyle competitions at Nashoba. I was no stranger to throwing flat spins and semi-inverted tricks on fifty-foot jumps. There's nothing quite like sailing off a jump into space and playing like a bird in the wind. And when you nail your trick, it feels even better.

Nashoba is our winter home-away-from-home. No wonder Mom wanted me to spend the day there—it's our safe place—but Eric's place was so much closer, and it was where I hit my first big tricks. I had landed my first backflip a week earlier in The Wasteland. Eric and I GoPro'd everything we did, and Paul did the editing. He made an "evolution of Jack's backflip" video—I still have it—of me failing badly my first time, improving it on the next two attempts, and then nailing it on the fourth. The video went viral with our friends on Facebook, and even my teachers asked me about it at school. All of this added to my sense of invincibility.

What's next? What's my next trick? Anything, as far as we were concerned, was possible. Paul soon landed his backflip, and Eric nailed the blind spin we call a backside 360. Every day we pushed ourselves.

By midafternoon on the sixteenth, we had done ten runs and I only had another run or two left in me. It was time to do the backflip again. I was now doing one at the end of every day, partly because it felt so good, and partly because I was afraid I'd forget how.

But then I thought about doing something different. There was one trick I'd been thinking about for years. *Why the hell not?* It was time to nail the frontside rodeo.

I had built a cannon box off to the side, a few feet above a cutout in the hill, so I could get more air. The more height you get, the more time you have to play with. And I needed height because the frontside rodeo adds a spin to the backflip. It's a 540-degree rotation (360 plus 180, one and a half turns) from takeoff to landing.

Why's it called a cannon box? Because the board angles up at the end, sending you higher and giving you more hang time. When you hit it hard it's like being shot out of a cannon.

If it's built right, that is.

I made the run and hit that frontside rodeo about ten times, but only in my head. I sat in the snow by the shed for five minutes, thinking it over. I was visualizing the run and breathing deep to soothe the nerves.

Nerves are good. They keep you awake and on your toes. That's their job.

I knew I had to go in with knees bent like springs, every fiber in my legs ready to explode. I knew I had to keep my head turned and my eyes on the landing all the way through the 540. Sitting there, I imagined every possible outcome—except one—and was nervous enough to even think about blowing it off. I had only recently nailed the backflip and now I was going to add a spin? But I was never the kid to back down from anything, and this was only a little harder than all the other tricks I'd done. Worst case scenario, I'd fall flat on my face. My face could take it, I figured.

The boys and I knew that if I were to land this or even come close on my first try, it would be beautiful.

Snowboarding is a weird way to travel. It's more like a fun way to fall. Gravity pulls you downhill, and you fall the whole length of the mountain to the lift line so you can do it again. You fall and hope the falling happens on your feet. More likely, though, at least at the beginning, you travel part of the way on your face or butt.

With skiing, you have four points of contact with the snow—two skis, two poles—but with a board it's only one point, so you're pretty much just a mushroom swaying back and forth while trying to stay upright at high speed. The board is as happy going backward as forward, and if you catch an edge hard enough, you'll hit the snow faster than you can think. Anyone who wants to get into snowboarding has to be happy with falling and getting up, falling and getting up, all day long.

I've been falling my whole life. It comes with the territory. School is fine and my grades are good, but I'm a sports kid. Football, lacrosse, snowboarding, whatever. Sports are where I tested myself, where I proved I could push hard.

All through childhood I was obsessive about being the best at every sport I played. I threw lacrosse balls around in my yard until it was too dark to see. Then I put the lights on and did it some more. On the mountain, I snowboarded all day long and practiced my jumps and rails until I was exhausted. As I got into football, I watched hours of game film to improve myself and get ready for the competition. I took hits on the practice field so that I could get better at taking hits during a game.

I can't say I *loved* falling and getting up, but I do love what it's made me: a fighter.

I learned a lot of this from my dad, Bill Trottier. Dad grew up tough in Lowell, Massachusetts, and became a tough-love motivational father, someone rough and rugged on the outside, genuine and full-hearted and selfless on the inside. He's two hundred twenty-five pounds and built like a bear, but he's a bear who will do everything in his power to make you better, faster, stronger. Dad coached every youth team I was on and taught me how to be a man. He always said if I could hit the pillow at the end of a long day and know I'd given it my best shot, I'd succeed no matter how long it took. Dad is the one who carved into my brain the simple advice: don't be lazy.

And I'm not. I'm proud of how hard I play and how quickly I get up when knocked down. I'd been playing contact sports my whole life and couldn't count the stingers I'd had. I'd never broken a bone, but I'd been hurt a thousand times. Face plants and sore tailbones were part of every day on the snow. I hardly blinked when I got slammed or tackled in football. I'd knuckled lots of landings off big jumps at Nashoba and bumped and bruised every part of my body. What the hell could a little fall do that hadn't been done already?

I fall. I get up. That's what I do.

So finally, I just said, "Fuck it," and turned my board parallel to the hill. I slid down.

———————————

The biggest question in the world, and the hardest to answer: What if?

The audible snap you can hear on Paul's eight second video was the destruction of my C6 vertebra.

It turns out that a single vertebra is a fragile thing, like a Christmas ornament. Together, the vertebrae form a spine that is strong and flexible, a thing of beauty that protects those nerves that link the body to the brain. Crush it, as I did, and you can sever the ties that bind your body together. Shatter it, as I did, and everything changes.

My entire short life is in that *crack*, that pop in the audio signaling a break in what was a perfect white line of healthy spine. My childhood disappeared into the gap like water down a drain, and the question mark that is my adult life rose out of it like smoke.

═══════════════════════════

I'm not moving. Snowflakes drift past my nose, apparently more alive than I am.

But my brain is working; that's good. I'm lying down and not twisted up in pain; that's good too. I want to turn over, though, or at least sit up. I want to get up and shake it off. But that's definitely not happening. I'm sending the command out of my brain into . . . what? Into something that can't hear the asking.

But that cold something is my body. Roll over, shoulders! Push off the ground, arms! Pull me up, abs! All I want to do is turn over, just that little thing that even a dead leaf can do when the wind blows it down my street.

Snowflakes rotate and spin like dancers before melting into nothingness on my face.

A cloud of uncertainty forms inside me. Anxiety asks a question: What does this not-being-able-to-move mean? This is not me.

The universe is a big dark place, right? Roll your wheelchair outside tonight onto the lawn or driveway and look up past the lights at all that nothingness that surrounds this busy green and blue planet. The Earth is breathing and moving and making noise, and that's how we know what life is. Life grows and moves, and it moves with intent. Or as Bruce Lee put it, "Things live by moving and gain strength as they go."

In life, momentum is everything. That's what gives you speed to make decisions. Keep moving, and you can change direction. Stay still, and decisions are made for you.

This is as true emotionally as it is physically. Think positive thoughts, and you move forward. Worry, and you slow down. Fixate on your problems, and you're stuck.

Eric's hill is small and not very steep. There's not much momentum to gather, and any little glitch along the way—a bump, a soft spot, a hesitation—slows you down. As I pumped off the top of the slope and slid down for the frontside rodeo, my eyes were on the goal, my thoughts were positive, and my speed was as good as it had been for my backflips. Good enough, I figured.

Or not. The problem was my half-ass cannon box. The board sank into the snow, and I didn't get the lift I needed. As soon as I was in the air, I opened up my right shoulder and turned my head to the right and saw immediately that I hadn't gotten enough air. Without the push, I couldn't get the rotation. Without rotation, a flip is just a fail. My feet swung up over my head and stayed there.

I fell six feet straight down onto my neck and shoulder.

For as long as I live, I'll never forget the first few seconds after impact.

As soon as I hit the ground, I felt my arms and legs suddenly straighten out and lock into place, as if a key had been clicked in the back of my neck to turn me into a mannequin.

Thankfully, it only lasted a moment, but it was my first flash of feeling what it's like to be locked inside my body.

But I didn't know that then. All I knew was that I had zero momentum. After sliding downhill a little ways, I came to a stop and lay there.

From a distance, I'm sure I looked peaceful, resting. But I was frozen in place, just another fallen object in an endless blanket of fresh snow, ten inches deep and getting deeper.

Soon there was motion swirling around me. Slow at first, with Eric walking up the hill and Paul coming over to kneel at my side. Paul had watched the whole thing through the camera lens, and now that he knelt beside me, he saw the reality behind the image. He was the first to be worried, and neither his words nor his tone did much to comfort me.

"Jack, breathe. Breathe, Jack."

"Yeah, I'm good. I'm good." And I thought I was. I never lost consciousness. Things were weird, but at no point was I ever really scared. I wanted a few seconds to clear my head before standing up. When those few seconds, then more, went by and I still couldn't move, I didn't panic. Why would I panic if I didn't think it was serious?

Both of the guys asked me if I was alright. I said I was.

We talked a little about what went wrong on the jump, as we did every other time one of us missed a trick. We wanted to figure it out and do better the next time.

It seems odd now, but I was the one keeping the guys calm. Especially Eric, who was beginning to stress out. I spoke quietly, assuring him that it was only another stinger, that I'd get up soon.

"I just need a minute to regroup," I said, "but it's not that bad."

I kept using that regroup line until the ambulance came.

I still felt like there was a way for me to walk off the hill. Call it denial, I guess, but mainly it was ignorance. I knew about paralysis, but that was something that happened to other people. Even as I lay there unable to get up or move my legs, I didn't consider that possibility. I'm not sure that anyone, in the first moments after their life suddenly changes, believes it has happened to them.

I had managed to put my hands on my stomach, but only my biceps and shoulders were responding to my brain. It wasn't enough.

My jacket had slid up and covered my mouth, making it difficult to breathe. I tried and tried to unzip my jacket—I could put my hands in the right place, but none of my fingers were moving. I asked Paul to do it. He definitely saw that I couldn't use my fingers but didn't say anything.

We weren't doing much talking now. Eric was standing beside me, waiting for me to get up while Paul went back to the video, replaying it to try to understand what happened.

I could feel Eric just standing there.

"It's not that bad," I told him. "Give me a minute."

Eric and Paul made eye contact, but neither one knew what to say. They had confidence in my confidence, I guess, and mostly we were just three teenage boys who did more playing than talking.

After a few minutes, frustration set in and I was anxious to get back up. I figured sitting up would help me get my head straight, so I asked Paul and Eric to pull me up.

Huge mistake. What I didn't know was that I had pieces of a shattered vertebra pressing against my spinal cord and any motion could cause more swelling, which destroys nerves. I also didn't know that it can take up to two years for the swelling to come down.

What I did know was that I instantly became lightheaded and my vision started to fade. Remember that kid's game where someone spins you around a bunch of times and then you try to walk in a straight line? Well, this dizziness was much worse, plus some nausea. I took some deep breaths to keep from throwing up and had the guys lower me back down.

I knew also that I needed medical attention. I needed it now.

I couldn't feel anything from my chest down. My legs had apparently fallen asleep. My hands were starting to hurt from the tingling. As I sank into the snow, I knew I needed to act fast. I could see in Eric's eyes how nervous he was for me. Minutes were ticking by, and he was getting more and more stressed.

Which makes what happened next kind of funny.

"I need help, man. Like now."

"Yeah, Jack, anything you need. What do I do?"

"You're going to have to call 911."

"No, you're not going to need that."

Wait, what? Eric was in shock, as was Paul. I had crossed that line too. My body was weakening, and it was hard to stay awake. Shocks to body and mind. Nobody wanted to call but it needed to be done. Eric wavered, then decided to run up to the house and ask his mom for help.

While he took off running, I was fading but wanted to make one last effort to feel something below my chest. Besides, the last thing I wanted was Eric's mom to find me lying there helpless. I asked Paul to unstrap my board and take it off. I closed my eyes and used all my might to send a signal down to my feet to feel what was going on. No luck.

When I opened my eyes, the board was already off.

That was a really shitty moment. I no longer had nerves to

keep me on my toes.

Eric and his mom were moving fast as they came out of the house. Eric had told me that she had been worried about something like this happening ever since we built our terrain park. I could hear the fear in her voice as she approached.

This was the first time I'd met Mrs. Vadenais, strangely enough. I'd spent a ton of hours in The Wasteland working on new tricks but had never talked with her. Now without introductions she was rushing in to take care of me.

But I couldn't see her. My hood blocked my view. There was only her voice, her stressed-out voice, as she stood off to the side.

But it felt good to have an adult there. I understood Eric's need to translate the weirdness of this situation through his mother rather than calling 911 himself. The shock, the paralysis, the decisions were all in an adult's hands, and it was comforting to have that voice in charge.

Not that I heard much of it. I remember hearing Mrs. Vadenais on the phone, but I had no idea what she was saying. I was busy trying to stay afloat. Everything was fading away except the confusion. How could I have fallen from just six feet—the height of a man—and been laid out like a corpse in rigor mortis, motionless, drifting away in my mind?

She kept asking me if I was okay. I kept saying yes. And once or twice I gave her my "I need a minute to regroup" line, but it was starting to sound a little shaky.

"Keep your eyes open. Try to stay awake," Mrs. Vadenais said. "Eric, make sure he stays awake." It's funny, but I don't even think she knew my name. I heard what she was saying, but I couldn't respond. The shock was going deep, and I was slurring my words. All I wanted to do was close my eyes and doze off.

My body is a weight, a sinking ship, falling slowly through darker and darker waters. As I reach the bottom, the last thing I notice is the feel of each cold inch of snow against my back, cupping my body like a soft, cruel bed.

I was still pretty calm as I faded, but my thinking was less and less clear. I knew I should notify my family and remembered that my mother had left her phone at home, but I couldn't turn the options I was considering into words. Shock was doing to my speech what the accident had done to my legs.

Paul took the initiative and called my sister, Sam, at Nashoba. Eric's mom took a deep breath and called my father. Neither conversation was easy, I'm sure.

I never understood a word. I knew my family would be concerned and would do whatever was necessary to help. That was more than enough to soothe me at the moment. I was lost in the falling flakes of my snowy dream world.

Something else was going on, too. Most of my drifting away was shock, but part of it was talent. I mean that I've always been good at mentally tuning out and moving on when the situation requires it. I'm the sort of person who in the middle of something horrible can shut out the emotions and instead think about something fun from the third grade. In this case, the few thoughts still floating through my mind were not about my injury. I was planning my weekend and hoping to talk with a girl I liked at school.

I woke to the sound of sirens. In the few sunken, blissful moments I'd been away, I had completely forgotten where I was.

An ambulance, a fire truck, and a few cop cars gathered at

the bottom of the hill. Other than the sirens, though, it was still a pretty quiet winter scene. No one else had driven on the road since I showed up a few hours earlier.

It's funny how in a crisis you can be bothered by the little things. I live in Tyngsboro, Massachusetts, a small town of eleven thousand people where I feel like I know everyone, but the first voice I heard was a police officer who I didn't recognize. Not sure why it bugged me, except that I guess we all prefer to be rescued by people we know.

The officer was the first on scene. He quickly saw how serious it was and told the EMTs to bring a backboard.

This was when the world became too busy for me to keep up. One EMT asked me questions—"Can you move your legs? Can you squeeze my hand? Can you feel this?"—while the others made a plan. Because my answers were all no, they knew it was serious. But they were quick and efficient, and they kept calm, which kept me calm.

"Keep your eyes open, Jack. Stay awake so we can talk to you."

"Okay, no problem."

"Great. Now, are you lightheaded or in any pain?"

And so it went, with me swerving in and out of awareness.

Finally, the EMTs told me to take deep breaths to calm my heart rate while they wrapped a foam pad around my head to stabilize my neck, tipped me up to slide the backboard underneath me, strapped me down, and arranged for four people to lift the board and carry me down to the ambulance.

It was fifteen minutes from their arrival to my departure.

Meanwhile, Paul was showing the video of my fall to two officers. It was strange to open my eyes and see them watching it closely as I was being readied for transport. Like I was already gone, in some kind of bubble, even though my body was right there next to them. Part of me—the old Jack, I guess—was trapped in the camera, and part of me—the confused and injured Jack—was moving on.

I have to admit that in my exhaustion there was something nice about decisions being made for me. I was headed off into the unknown, but for now I could close my eyes and be lost somewhere between my calm place and unconsciousness.

This is when my life story changed. It was no longer *Three Guys with Snowboards and a GoPro Do Something Epic*. This is when it became *Jack in the New World*. As the sirens cried out, and as Paul and Eric and Mrs. Vadenais and The Wasteland faded in the distance through the ambulance window, I wondered what was next.

═══════════════

My head is pinned like a dead insect, I can't feel my legs, and the taste of vomit coats my mouth. I'm anxious and shocked and tired and nauseous and afraid. My heart is pounding and my brain, I think, is on fire.
What the hell kind of fun snow day is this?

Sleep was both my greatest desire and the least likely option. With my body rocking back and forth as the ambulance wound along the roads between Tyngsboro and Lowell General Hospital, and my stomach trying to come up for air, I needed a distraction.

I tried to entertain my new companion.

"Do you think you could cancel my dentist appointment for me?"

I don't know if the paramedic knew I was joking—he made

some small noise to answer me—and really, I don't even know if it was a joke. (I mean, is it a joke if nobody laughs?)

I've always dealt with pain through humor. It changes the topic and gives me a little control over the situation. Jokes seem perfect when things are awkward or difficult.

That said, I don't know how I would have felt if the EMT had laughed. Yes, I like it when people chuckle at my jokes, but I was happy to have him focus on my vital signs. His job was to keep me alive. No comedy required.

But this guy seemed nervous, almost scared. It was like he thought I was going to die and couldn't hide his fear. So I offered him a chance to lighten up, for my sake at least.

His lack of response made me even more uneasy.

And I felt really, really uneasy. Sure, something weird had happened to my body and I had no idea how bad it was, but what was killing me was dizziness and nausea. I'd tasted it on the hill, but it hit me like a wave as soon as we started down the road. I get carsick a lot, and that's without being strapped down and riding backward in an ambulance with bad shocks and a stench of fear and cleaning chemicals. Add three super-bright lights above me so I can't open my eyes, throw in a terrified paramedic for company, and race me around the narrow, congested streets of downtown Lowell, and it's a safe bet I'm going to fill up some of your sick bags. Which is what I did. The poor guy had to lift one side of the backboard each time I threw up.

All I wanted was to make it to the hospital and be put under so I could escape my mind.

Misery does not like company.

I need to be clear about this. I hate hospitals. Let me count the ways. First—irony intended—hospitals make me ill. Second, they're full of sick people, hurt people, dying people. So why would I want to hang out there?

And ambulances are just hospital rooms on wheels. Bouncy, smelly, claustrophobic, vomit-filled hospital rooms.

There was one breath of fresh air on this first journey, and it was literally a breath of fresh air. At Lowell General, the ambulance doors opened, and a cold January gust burst in and settled my stomach almost immediately. It was nearly five in the evening, and the snow had finally stopped.

The only other good memory I have of Lowell happened about ten seconds later, under the heat lamps stationed outside the ER entrance. The paramedics had thrown a blanket on me, but the warmth emanating from the heat lamps was amazing. Maybe it was my addled mind or maybe I was grateful to be out of the vomit bus, but I'd never seen outdoor heat lamps before, and they gave me such a moment of comfort and happiness. It was like stepping into a warm bath. They made so much sense on a twenty-degree night to a miserable person on a gurney. I hope whoever thought of putting them outside the ER entrance got some kind of humanitarian award.

My brief dose of paradise ended as we passed through the hospital doors. All I could see were things directly above me, which were mostly white ceilings and lights. I wish hospitals wrote "Welcome!" and other nice messages on the ceiling for arriving patients, but instead there were only signs on the walls that pointed the way to Emergency, Trauma, Heart, and Vascular.

I was the ball on a roulette wheel: *Ladies and gentlemen, place your bets! Where will Jack stop?* Which door was mine? I still didn't know what was wrong with me. As far as I knew it could be my heart or brain. I didn't even know how paralysis happened.

And the ball stopped on: trauma.

One definition of trauma is "a serious injury or shock to the body, as from violence or an accident." Check.

Oh wait, there's also this: "An emotional wound or shock that creates substantial, lasting damage to the psychological development of a person." Yes, that's what I've been wrestling with ever since that day, like any teenager who drops out of the sky into a wheelchair.

But let's fade to black for now. Because looking up at the Trauma sign is where my solid memories of Lowell end. I'd made it to the hospital. I didn't have to fight to stay awake anymore. Something inside me, a tension, finally relaxed. I blacked out.

But before I pass out on the page here, I want to mark a moment. Officially I want to recognize it and call it what it is. A little after three p.m. on January 16, 2013, I turned my life upside down. Everything that's happened since has been about landing on my feet.

2

BOSTON

Life is strange. And cold. I'm exhausted and trapped and afraid.

It's hard to describe exactly how terrifying it is to be lying on a hospital bed before a major surgery on a mysterious injury while your parents stand next to you with tears running down their faces.

All the scary near-death hospital scenes from TV shows and movies were always someone else's stories I watched or decided not to watch before changing the channel. Now there was no escaping it. I was the story.

I said "near-death" but maybe it's worse than that.

Am I dying?

Lowell turned out to be a one-hour stopover on a greater journey to Boston and a deeper journey into trauma medicine. I woke up for a moment in a cold MRI room, long enough to have a foggy conversation with a doctor about how the injury was too much for Lowell General to handle. They wanted to transfer me to Boston Children's Hospital, and did they have my permission? I said, "Yes," not sure what to think.

Good news: I was headed to a bigger, better facility. Bad news: What was so complicated?

I needed sleep, but more importantly I needed a strategy. It's hard to tune out and move on when you're also wondering what the hell is going on. Things were overwhelming me. I still didn't know what was happening, but I knew it was serious. Really serious.

My dad often told me, "Feel the fear, but do it anyway." Failure is often the first step to success and trying is everything.

I was definitely feeling the fear now, though it was a vague storm beneath my exhaustion. What was I supposed to do? What was my fight, my challenge? What obstacle was I supposed to push through?

For now, all I could do was try to keep my spirits up.

But that was easier said than done. I was Alice gone down the rabbit hole strapped to a backboard and staring at the ceiling. I'd been launched into what felt like someone else's story, a different reality.

It was a movie. That's what it felt like. I was an actor in a strange movie. My job was to improvise the character's lines because no one gave me a script.

My character was partly me, partly my fear. I like to tell jokes and smile, and my fear, like I said before, prefers funny to painful, so I guess I was being typecast. But it was a role I could sell. And so, as much as possible, I became the Cheerful Patient.

My first performance was during the evening ambulance ride

to Boston. What did I feel? Extreme nausea—puking all over the steel floor—and disoriented and blurry and like I was in a bad dream that wouldn't end. How did I act? Open-eyed and smiling. Well, at least until I blacked out again right before we got to Boston Children's.

It would be a little while until I got the role figured out.

I woke up in another sterile room—farther down the rabbit hole—but this time was different. I could sense that there were people in the room with me. Not just hospital people, but people people.

As my eyes began to focus, I saw my mom and dad standing on the left side of my bed. I want to say I felt a flood of relief at the sight of their faces, and so I will: it was a relief to see them. But it only took a moment to see that the tears on my mother's face were not tears of joy at our reunion but tears for me. For whatever might happen.

I was in a presurgery holding room.

I tried not to get too anxious, but it wasn't easy. I looked around the room for a distraction and saw my clothes on the table. For a second, I could set aside matters of life, death, grief, and confusion and wonder, *Hey, wait, they took my underwear off?*

But I had a bigger question tumbling around my mind. It was a question I did not want to ask. I could only look around the room trying not to ask it for so long, though. I couldn't stop the question any more than I could predict the answer.

With my eyes starting to tear up I turned to my mom and looked straight at her. She knew what I was going to ask even before I opened my mouth, but I looked her dead in the eyes and asked it anyway.

"Am I going to be okay?"

Her expression went from upset to hysterical to comforting all in a split second. I literally watched her get hit with a wave of sadness and fear. Her eyes got big and watery, and then she quickly composed herself.

"Yes, everything is going to be fine, Jack." She put on a brave face and smiled, all while trying her best not to bawl her eyes out. What was weird, and a bit chilling, was that the scene played out exactly like you'd expect it to in a movie.

Reality was feeling a bit shaky.

I wanted to believe my mom. I still felt like maybe in a day or two I could be walking out of the hospital back to my actual life. So, for verification, I took a look over at my dad.

Oh shit.

Dad was looking down at his clasped hands, and his face was wet with tears. In the seventeen years between my hospital birth and this hospital crisis, I have seen my dad cry only a couple times, and this was one of them. If he was crying, then something serious was going on. This wasn't just another break or sprain on the football field.

We were silent for a long time after that. I shut my eyes. I couldn't handle it. This was not a Cheerful Patient scene where positive talking pushes away negative thinking. This was a genuine maybe-I'm-about-to-die low point.

And that's the problem with silence, to be honest. Sometimes important things go unsaid, like, for instance, that I wasn't about to die. It might have been funny if we'd talked about it right then, as in "Wait, you guys aren't crying because I might not survive surgery? Why didn't I know that?"

They say comedy is tragedy plus time, and in that room time stood still. My parents were standing there suffering, wondering if their son would ever walk again. Still woozy from shock and confused by my parents' fear, I was lying there wondering if I'd go into surgery and never wake up again. All the friends and family I might never see, and all the people I never got a chance to say goodbye to: that's the grief I couldn't handle.

I tried my best to hold back the tears. I didn't feel like talking to anyone. I don't know if I could have talked, honestly. I didn't know what I was feeling, and I didn't know if I had the words to express whatever the feelings might be.

Everything was unreal.

This part of the movie really sucked.

I was so far gone, actually, that it felt like a nightmare. Most of my body was numb and unresponsive, my head and neck were locked down to keep them stable, my parents were weeping, and I was about to be operated on for a condition that I thought might end my life. This is when I first understood what terror means: naked fear, constant threat, no control.

I had zero experience with this kind of stress. It just felt like my brain was being attacked. It had only been a few hours, but I was so far out of my comfort zone that I'd forgotten what regular life felt like.

Finally I couldn't control it, and tears slowly streamed down my face.

I remember almost nothing that happened between this breakdown and when I woke up after surgery.

I can reconstruct the scene, though, from what I was told afterward.

My surgeon, Dr. Proctor, came in to tell my parents what he needed to do—cut into my neck as soon as possible and take out the bone fragments putting pressure on my spinal cord—and that he required their permission to do it. He didn't want to wait for an MRI because decompressing the spinal cord was the first priority. They signed off immediately, and I was taken into the OR at eight p.m.

There are thirty-three vertebrae in a human spine, in five sections: cervical, thoracic, lumbar, sacral, and coccygeal. Nerves from around the body feed into the spine at different vertebrae to connect with the brain. Higher spine injuries paralyze more of the body because more of those nerves lose that connection. *Cervical* is the *C* in C6, which is the sixth vertebra down from the skull. Damage to nerves at the C6 level can cause, you guessed it, paralysis in the legs, torso, and hands. There are other complications, too, but I'm not ready to talk about that.

My parents weren't offered any particular diagnosis in terms of recovery. One spinal injury can walk out of the hospital after a week, another will be wheelchair-bound for life. So doctors say "*might* not walk again," never "*will* not walk again." At least they did with me.

The surgical team put me under, stuck a breathing tube down my throat, and made a three-inch incision through the skin, fat, and muscle on the front right side of my neck. The surgeon then opened the incision with retractors to create a window onto my damaged spine.

Here's what they saw: the disc between C5 and C6 was completely blown out, and the C6 vertebra was broken so that some pieces were deeply embedded into the spinal cord. Dr. Proctor, looking through an operating microscope, extracted the pieces of the vertebra as well as the C5-C6 and C6-C7 discs above and below it. He implanted a one-inch piece of donor fibula bone to fill the gap and then screwed a two-inch plate to both my C5 and C7 vertebrae to hold it all together. After four hours, Dr. Proctor closed up the incision with dissolving stitches and some glue, which peeled off later.

Luckily, by the time I woke I was breathing on my own and they had taken out the tube. I think if I'd woken up gagging on a tube, I might have flipped out. I mean, I suppose I'd be happy to be alive once I thought about it a bit, but that might have taken a while. It was weird enough to have no feeling in most of my body and to have a brace snugged around my neck.

I still have a love/hate relationship with the memory of the surgery. To get such advanced care so quickly is a blessing I can't ever say enough about, but it's hard for me even to think about what's in my neck and what they had to do to put it there. I'm not even that fond of looking at the scar, I have to say. I guess when it comes to being cut open, I'm a bit of a wimp.

━━━━━━━━━━

What a weird, deep dream. It went on forever. Something about landing upside down in Eric's yard, then ambulance rides and throwing up, then doctors and nurses and a hospital—no, wait, two hospitals—and some kind of crazy surgery on my neck. I think I was paralyzed. Mom and Dad were there, and they were crying, and the last thing I remember was going into surgery.

Why does my room smell so strange? Why am I sleeping on my back? Whatever. I need to open my eyes now and get up.

Oh no.

What I woke to, as we all do every day, was the rest of my life.

This would be a cliché if the rest of my life didn't look so strange and hard.

And speaking of clichés, I actually thought, as my brain crawled out from beneath the anesthesia, that everything from the frontside rodeo to the C6 spinal fusion surgery had been a crazy dream. The accident and ambulances, the stress and surgery: I had one delicious minute when I thought the nightmare would fade with the sleepiness.

The sadness that came after that minute has kept me company off and on ever since.

It wasn't any easier for my parents. I don't remember this, but my mom told me later that after the surgery my parents were allowed in to see me. She was crying as I went in and out of consciousness. But she got herself together and sat down close beside me and said, "Jack, I will never leave you. I will always be with you."

I managed to croak out a weak and choppy "Thank you," but my throat was raw from the breathing tube and my mind was far away. The words came out on a weird, deflating breath. Mom said those two words were so chilling that they'll stick with her forever.

The whirlwind of my first day was replaced by a silence marked by a series of long hard examinations of the blank ceiling. Family and other visitors came and went, and I slept a lot, but other than that I had a lot of time to think about things.

You know that famous line about "the only thing we have to fear is fear itself?" I was in that hospital bed staring at the ceiling and literally fearing the fear. I was afraid to let it in; I was afraid for the future; I was just plain afraid. I wasn't even entirely sure what to be afraid of yet, but it was haunting me anyway.

And when I wasn't fearing fear, I had begun to obsess over what went wrong in The Wasteland. It turns out there are at least a million ways to slide down a small hill on a snowboard. There are even more ways to push off and spin through the air. I have done them all. In some ways I'm still that kid sitting at the top of the hill planning his run, but in one terrible way I am still that same kid lying in the snow still trying to figure out what happened.

That first day of recovery in the ICU at Boston Children's, I tried not to think about it, but I had to. While a whole team of great nurses and doctors came in and out of the room with water or a warm blanket or to reset the beeping equipment I was plugged into, I had to relive it, to play it over and over in my head, so maybe I could make peace with it.

And to be honest, not thinking about it is still a challenge. Hardly a day goes by in which I don't think about that launch off the cannon box, about what happened in midair, about how it could have gone differently.

There are so many reasons why it's terrible for me to think about what I could or should have done. For one, it doesn't help. For another, to quote King Lear, "that way madness lies."

"Live in the present" is the wisdom we all struggle to achieve. But I was starting to wonder what my present was. Was it this moment in the hospital with IVs and morphine drips and the "blah, blah, blah" of the TV? Or was it the past and its endless unrealized variations that haunted me? Because that past was playing through my mind on repeat, and pretty much any moment in a hospital feels like Limbo.

Hours felt like days; days felt like years. Days full of lying in a bed and sinking into the mattress like I sank into the snow on Eric's hill, except I was starting to feel like I had stopped sinking and had simply sunk. This was bottom.

Was this bottom? Whatever it was, I was doped up and sharing it with whatever visitor was by my side: mom, dad, sister, brother, cousin.

And, apparently, a famous Boston Bruin. Bob Sweeney of the Bruins Foundation showed up one day when I was so dazed on pain meds that I couldn't speak. I hardly remember him being there. He was kind enough to bring a jersey and hat signed by all the Bruins, but I was in such a fog that all I could think about was a single question rattling around my brain: *How did he hear about me?*

My story, I found out later, had been broadcast around Massachusetts the day after it happened. A few days later, my father was interviewed on the local CBS station and my brother Ian and his wife Angela were on Fox 25. Tens of thousands of people were hearing what happened to me while I was motionless in my hospital bed. I was glad that the big stuff like news broadcasts were happening, but for me it was the little stuff that was the most real.

Like on day three, when I had a real shock. The good news was that I was allowed to have solid food again. The better news was that it was homemade shepherd's pie, my favorite. The bad news was that none of us had thought ahead for this moment. No one said, "Hey, Jack can't hold a spoon anymore. What's our plan?" Come dinnertime, my dad and I looked at each other, then admitted the obvious. He was going to have to feed me.

Each tasty spoonful just seemed cruel. After realizing I was paralyzed, this was the next real "oh shit" moment.

═══════════════

Sometimes it's the little things that keep us going when we feel like giving up. It's like rock climbing, when you look

up at a giant cliff or boulder and know you can survive
by finding little bits of rock for your fingers and toes. It
doesn't take much.

I'm lying here in this hospital bed as a genuine victim
of gravity, but I also know that gravity can be overcome as
long as you have something to hold on to. For me, some-
times a smile is as good as a handhold.

Having Ian around helped me cope with reality. Ian is my half-brother, but I never think of him as half-anything. He's my brother, fourteen years older, my dad's son. As a kid, I didn't see him a lot, but it was always fun for me when we were together. We became close on that Colorado ski trip when I first fell in love with terrain parks. I was eight years old. On the chairlift, just the two of us, he gave me permission to curse, and I became the happiest foul-mouthed second grader you ever saw. It was supposed be a secret between brothers, but of course that night in the condo when someone talked about how much they hated it when the chairlift stopped halfway up the mountain, I said, "I know, that's fucking annoying."

Which really didn't go over well with my dad. But it's been funny for a long time.

When Ian showed up in the ICU, I wanted to have a little fun. I think I also wanted to show him I was still me, that my head was still in a good place. When Dad stepped out of the room, I told Ian what I was about to do.

The problem was I was going to have to hold my breath for a good amount of time. And maybe pass out. But it would be worth it.

When Dad came back, Ian got him talking while I sat there

quietly. After a few seconds, the machine that monitored my breathing started to ding. Every two seconds or so, as I continued to hold my breath, it got louder. DING. And louder. DING, DING. After twenty seconds or so it had reached full volume. Dad heard the noise and went from smiling to having a fairly serious look to wide eyes. He looked at me, then up to the monitor, then back to me.

It's tough to get a reaction out of my father, so this was pretty good. He looked at me again and gave me a quick "Jack?" Getting no reaction, he jumped for the door to find a nurse. By now the monitor was clanging, and the alarm light outside my door was lit up.

I took a big breath in, then shouted, "DAD!"

He turned and looked at me with a serious look only one step from the door. Ian was cracking up, and I had a smile on my face. He gave me those I'm-going-to-kill-you eyes that I get periodically throughout my life, and then he gave those eyes to my brother. Then he sighed and shook his head. He seemed quietly happy to see me screwing around again. I was still his son.

The smile on my face is, in general, the only solution I found to the problem King Lear talks about: the madness that comes with obsessing over his worries. Lear decides he can't think about it anymore. Me too. But I needed to do more than that. I couldn't leave part of myself on that hill; I couldn't think about what I might have done. Eventually, I had to move on to other things. And honestly, I just feel better if I'm smiling and joking through my day. I think it helps us all get through our crap a little easier.

Maybe the smile on my face will help get me back on my feet, and if not, then I'll go down smiling. I want to say, "Hey, a life with new challenges every day is a life worth living," even if those challenges sometimes feel unbeatable. It's easy to say, I know, but maybe overcoming challenges is the whole point of life? And when the challenge is close to impossible, maybe the fight is the victory?

So maybe I'm Sisyphus instead of Alice. I'll push and push my rock up the hill and then do it again. But there are moments when things are so strange that I feel like Alice again. Maybe I can be both? It's funny to think of Sisyphus meeting the Mad Hatter or Alice rolling the stone up the hill.

Either way, I see myself as a fighter. It's not about how hard the fight is but how hard I try.

===========

I am not fighting. I am not pushing. I am losing; I am lost. I am in agony.

The pain explodes in my head, and I nearly pass out. It's four in the morning, and I just woke up with my head shattered. A nurse is cleaning out the blood pressure medication IV with saline, and I'm begging her to stop. Then the pain is so intense I can't speak or think. I can only focus on the excruciating pain. There is nothing else but the pain. If I do talk, I slurrr-mmmyy-wworrds. I am desperate to grab the bedrails, but even that relief has been stolen from me because my fingers don't work. My hands slide uselessly along the steel.

Imagine your car goes off the cliff and someone yells "Hold on!" but that someone is you and the car is your body in pain and there's nothing to hold.

I wait for it to end. The exploding becoming throbbing, which, after about ten minutes, slowly seeps away, leaving me a wreck.

Saline flushes are common practice. They happened twice every day during my stay in Boston, and each time it felt like I was being tortured. Nobody really knew why. Apparently, I was an anomaly. A really miserable anomaly.

Almost as bad as the pain was the anticipation. If I wasn't asleep, and I saw the nurse show up with saline and a syringe to flush the IV, my stomach would drop. I watched and waited and felt the pain coming on fast like a swinging hammer, and all I could do was wait it out, suffering until I could start to breathe again.

No one was trying to hurt me, I knew, and the cause of the pain was so innocuous—a little saline in the IV, nothing more—but that misery burned itself into my brain.

I will never forget the feeling. It could wake me from a dead sleep. First the smell, then a cooling sensation in my arm, then the headache. A wave of nausea too. All I wanted was to quietly breathe through the pain without anything touching me. But with every heartbeat my head throbbed, and with every throb I blinked, almost like the headache was rattling my brain.

The smell. Just a little salty water, right? But the sensation was bizarre. Imagine your nose being stuffed with snow, but a little salty. Kind of like sea-snow. Is that a thing? A saltwater snowstorm in my nose, with thunder inside my head.

The nurses' best guess was that my nervous system was freaking out because of the spinal cord injury. Maybe little changes triggered big reactions. They did their best to ease me through it—a cold compress on my face helped but made me claustrophobic and anxious—and after a while we all figured this pain had to take its own course. Nobody had the answers.

I was starting to think that every stage of my misery would be matched by another level of weirdness. Sisyphus, meet Alice.

Which brings me to phantom feeling and nerve pain. People who lose sensation in their limbs begin to feel a ghost war going on beneath their skin. I could feel the presence of my legs, but I couldn't feel the surface. That's phantom feeling. On the inside, however, I felt more than I could handle. That was the nerve pain. My nervous system was in chaos, every few minutes firing off lightning bolts down the side of my body all the way to my toes with a quick zap.

As an athlete I constantly bounced back from bruises and sprains. I knew something about controlling pain, about developing an attitude that ignores and reduces pain to a certain extent. This lightning, though, was being generated inside my body. I didn't know where it was coming from or why it hurt so much. Like my saline reaction, this nervous-system pain was extreme and sudden and strange. And like so much else in my new life, it was completely out of my control.

The doctors tried a few medications, which, sadly, couldn't touch the pain. So, they set up a morphine drip. The morphine suppressed the expression of pain in my nervous system by mimicking the endorphins a body produces to limit pain, increase sleepiness, and feel pleasure. I think we've all heard that morphine, the ancestor of heroin, is a seriously effective drug.

I was allowed a dose roughly every hour. All I needed to do to begin a dose was to press a button at my bedside. But like a bad joke, I was no more able to hit the button to get the morphine than I was to grip the bedrail when the saline racked my brain.

My morphine was not handicap accessible.

I had to call for help every time I wanted a dose. This killed me, because I had to admit one weakness just so I could get help for another weakness. Everything about this sucked.

But you know what sucked even more? The pain, which was hellacious.

The problem with an opiate like morphine, as centuries of addiction and death have demonstrated, is that it is as dangerous as it is effective. It's still sometimes used for injured troops in combat to slow their heart rate and limit pain signals to the brain. But on the battlefield, as in a hospital setting, there are very strict rules in place for how much and how often morphine can be given. Too big a dose, and the body forgets how to breathe.

At the beginning, a day or two after my surgery, I was being ravaged by the ferocious bolts of electricity setting fire to my nerves and putting my pain receptors on high alert. I kept calling the nurses every ten minutes, hoping for another dose.

Around seven p.m. one evening, during a nurse shift change, I had been given a hit of morphine, but my pain kept increasing. Everyone had been telling me how morphine begins to work instantaneously once it enters my veins, but my veins were telling me something different. The pain escalated, and I was once again reduced to begging for help. I wasn't able to hit the morphine button on my right, but I could hit the yellow call button with my left elbow. Even when a nurse showed up, though, I knew that real help wasn't coming.

But then a new face appeared. Shocked at my visible level of pain, this new nurse talked with a comforting voice while immediately swapping the empty container with a full one to begin a new drip. Even in my foggy, drugged-up mind I knew that it was too early for a new dose, but I didn't care. I needed relief.

And suddenly the pain subsided. My breathing slowed. I was thrilled and relaxed at the same time, if that's even possible. I was a new man. I was having normal thoughts rather than a constant battle with pain and anxiety.

It was perfect. I couldn't figure out why they didn't give me that dosage every time.

Until a few minutes later. Abruptly my new man began slipping under waves of unconsciousness. As my heart rate slowed, thanks to the morphine, my breathing slowed with it.

I was looking over to the right side of the room at a small window with the blinds drawn. Two parallel thoughts were running quietly through my brain: *I am calmly falling asleep for the first time in days*, and *I think I'm about to stop breathing.*

And I did. Both. I fell into a beautiful deep sleep, and I stopped breathing.

Then DING . . . I woke a few seconds later to the monitor above my head sounding through the hospital room, telling me to take a breath.

I did, then fell back asleep.

A few seconds later—DING—the alarm and a breath. Then again, and again, each time struggling to wake from a deeper and deeper sleep.

Then the alarm had no effect. I was out and down, unconscious, taking maybe four faint breaths a minute, just enough to stay alive.

I was still in the ICU, but in stable condition, so typically when an alarm went off in my room it was because one of my other medications had run out. Not a crisis, in other words. The light over my door would light up and a nurse would come in soon to take care of things.

Now the alarm—DING, DING, DING—was getting louder and louder, saying to anyone who could hear it that the situation was, "Important, important," and getting, "Serious, serious."

My mom had been sleeping in a visitor chair this whole time with her head leaning on my bed and her hand resting on my arm. She woke now to the sound of the alarm and the bustle of two nurses flowing into my room to figure out what was going on. There was a sense of urgency that spooked her. She asked questions that went unanswered, as they often did when the staff was figuring something out.

Neither the nurses nor I could tell her that I was okay, because I was unresponsive.

Dad got the sucker-punch version of the Jack's-not-breathing game, but Mom got the real thing.

Moments were passing.

Soon the nurses set up an IV of naloxone, otherwise known as Narcan, a drug used to quickly reverse the symptoms of an opiate overdose.

A minute later I came up like a drowning man who didn't know he'd gone swimming.

"What the fuck just happened?" I asked the nurse who had given me both the extra dose and the Narcan.

She neither blinked nor took offense. "You took a little too much medicine. You should be all set in a minute." Her nonchalance pissed me off even more than my confusion. I was irrational, lost somewhere between overdose and recovery, between pain and relief, between anger and what seemed like a near-death experience.

I don't know if she was pretending it wasn't a big deal to cover up the mistake or to protect me and my mother from thinking too much about how close I had come to dying. Or maybe she really didn't think it was a big deal. Maybe it happens all the time. Nurses know a hell of a lot more about the nearness of death than I do.

But now I knew a little bit. I knew a lot more about pain and loss and grief and mortality than I wanted to.

Not that I'm complaining. The nurses at Boston Children's Hospital were amazing and, as far as I'm concerned, were going above and beyond to save my life the entire time I was there. This was the intensive care unit, so the stakes were high for every patient they cared for. The overdose was a shock, but just one of a thousand problems the ICU nurses solved every day.

The whole ordeal lasted maybe ten minutes. Only ten minutes, but I felt like I had reached some new dimension, some *Inception*-type weirdness, and I wish I could have filmed the descent I made into that twilight zone of No Pain and Endless Sleep, where nothing whatsoever was going through my head except the faint echo of a question—*What's happening to my body?*—before total silence took over.

I had been begging for a nothingness to sink into. And my prayer was answered. When I think back, I can still feel the pain subsiding and my eyes becoming heavy. It was beautiful. But the nothingness was too deep.

And so, I was back in the world of pain and inadequate relief, which was good, if difficult, news.

3

KEEP THE FAITH

Who am I now? Am I still the same Jack Trottier or his shadow?

What's my story? Am I a small-town football star turned cripple? A cautionary tale? A young man struggling against a life-changing injury?

Even if I'm not asking these questions out loud, why does no one have the answers?

Am I a fighter? A loser? Too soon to tell, I guess. Either way, I'm wounded and leaving my friends and family far behind.

A new day, a new dilemma: Where was I going for rehab? It had to happen right away, because the sooner therapy starts for a spinal cord injury, the better. I had been stuck in a hospital bed since the accident, and it was time to move again. The doctors told my parents about options here in Boston, in Pennsylvania, and even in Georgia. I would have been fine if they sent me to the dark side of the Moon.

Weightlessness sounded pretty good, actually.

Soon the conversation focused on the Shepherd Center in Atlanta, which they said was the best spinal cord and brain injury hospital in the country. They even had a special program for adolescent patients. "Best in the country" was all I needed to hear. I wanted to walk again. So it was goodbye Boston Children's, goodbye Tyngsboro, and goodbye to everything, really.

And it was a lot to say goodbye to, especially now that the word had gotten out about my accident. In the hospital, I was feeling trapped in my body and disconnected from ordinary life, and I wasn't sure how to reconnect. But now people were reaching out to me through messages and prayers and gifts, and I realized it wasn't only up to me to keep the connection.

My story had reached the entire greater Boston region in one night. And the community responded. Sam brought me my phone a day or two after surgery, and it was full of messages from family and neighbors and friends and from people I had never talked to in my life. It took days to read through all of it.

I couldn't hold my phone, so I asked Sam to read the messages. The feeling of listening to everybody's love being read out loud to you is hard to describe.

"Jack, we love you and are praying for you!"

"Come home soon, Jack. Tyngsboro isn't the same without you."

"Jack, you're amazing and strong! I know you can beat this!"

There were hundreds like that. Suddenly I knew that people would stand behind me no matter what happened.

That was a huge revelation. My eyes had been opened to how wide and kind the world can be. Listening to the blessings and good wishes made me realize that there are really good people in my life and in my little Massachusetts town.

Everyone should know what that feels like. Everyone. To feel connected and loved and part of a community that cares. It's a dream come true, even if we didn't know we had dreamed it before. The fact that this dream was coming true in the midst of a nightmare made it even more powerful.

I had allowed myself the luxury of having Sam read me all the messages, but I didn't want her to respond for me. I wanted to physically do it on my own. That was the first challenge I set for myself. Not being able to write back to people for days or even weeks would be tough, but it would motivate me. I needed the satisfaction of doing the work to thank them myself.

I couldn't put off saying my goodbyes, though. My two best friends, Derek and Justin, came to visit on my last day in Boston. Part of me didn't want them to see me like this, but the rest of me didn't care. I had to see my friends. If I was on a new journey, then I wanted them there with me.

Derek came strolling in first, tall and broad shouldered and wearing his green flannel. After some hellos and hugs, Mom and Dad and Sam cleared out so that I could hang out with him one-on-one. Even though family had been at my side, Derek felt like my first dose of reality from outside the white walls. I could see the excitement in his eyes, too, now that he was finally getting to see me. He'd been worried.

Still, he gave me his usual "What's up, buddy?" At first, all we could do was smile at each other. I couldn't move my arm to shake hands or sit up to hug, but it didn't matter. It was so good to see this face I'd known since we were little kids. We played sports together—football, lacrosse, and wrestling—our whole lives. We spent hours in the backyard shooting on the lacrosse net or throwing the football around. I actually started tearing up a little as I thought about how everything would be different now. We might never play sports together again.

We started with the easy stuff. Derek caught me up on the gossip back in Tyngsboro, which was mostly the crazy coincidence of my accident happening on the same day our friend Kyle was released from the hospital—after a bad car wreck—with staples in his head and a reattached ear. I told Derek more about my accident, but I also had to break my big news to him. "They think I should go to a special hospital in Atlanta. I'm going to be gone a while."

So simple, but so hard to say. I kept getting choked up, and there was a long moment where neither of us could really say anything. Telling my best friend that life had just gotten real, that I was going away, and it would be a long time before I got home or got better, was one of the hardest things I've ever had to do.

I guess saying it out loud made it even more real for me.

There was a knock on the door, so Derek stepped out to hang with my family as Justin came cruising in wearing his best white T-shirt. He was as upbeat as always. "Yo brotha, how are you?"

Again, all we could do was smile when he first stood next to my bed. For one thing, we both thought it was funny that his arm was in a cast and my neck was in a brace. I had been on the mountain with him when he'd snapped his wrist coming down short on a jump. Not a surprise, really. I've seen that kid fall hard so many times.

Justin was also a childhood friend, someone I did everything with—sports and sleepovers—and I loved our two seasons playing lacrosse together in high school. Those are memories I'll have forever.

And so is the memory of sitting there silently together after I told him I was going to Atlanta. For a moment, the only noise was the beeping heart rate monitor.

But it wasn't a painful silence. Despite the sadness of saying goodbye to Derek and Justin, I was feeling better and a little bit stronger now that I'd seen them. It took me a second to realize why. They had treated me exactly as if nothing had changed. They walked into the ICU like they were walking into my house to hang out. There was no hesitation or caution. I wasn't some new, strange Jack to them. I was just Jack, their friend. That meant a lot.

After a few minutes everyone else came back in. It was nice to have the room filled up with the warm sound of familiar voices. Best of all, I learned that Justin's dad would bring Derek and Justin down to Atlanta in a month, on March 2. That was an injection of hope shot straight into my heart. Knowing my friends would be there in a month made me think that maybe soon we could get back to the fun times we used to have. Maybe I'd be walking by then!

We couldn't hug, but first Derek and then Justin put their hand on my shoulder, looked me in the eyes, and wished me luck.

Right before they left we took a quick photo, with Justin on my left and Derek on my right, both of them leaning in next to me with big smiles and thumbs up. It's strange how a snapshot can take on so much meaning. For one thing, it was of my two best friends literally by my side after the worst days of my life. And it was the first picture to make it out after the accident, so it became a big deal on Facebook and everywhere else. Mainly, though, I think of that picture as day zero of my recovery. In a matter of hours, I was heading south.

Then at the end of the day, Sam had to leave too. She was on break from her freshman year at Marymount College in Manhattan, and she'd made the trip from work at Nashoba to the hospital every day since the accident. Having her there was important to me. Sam and I have always been close, and I've always been honest with her. In this moment of saying goodbye, though, the honesty felt heavy, like it was pinning me to my bed. It had been really nice to see my friends, but the lift I'd gotten had started to fade.

"I'm fucked, Sam." I shook my head and turned to look at her directly.

"You are *not*." Sam looked right back at me, calm and collected as always. She was sitting right by my bed, wearing one of her nice hipster sweaters. She has this quiet and gentle presence, which always calms me down.

"It will be okay, Jack. You'll see."

I could tell this wasn't a conversation she wanted to have. It was hard to see me like this, to see her brother hurt, to wonder what the future held for me and the family, but she stayed positive. Sam has never been one to make a speech, but she didn't need to. A few words from my older sister always made me feel a little better. She said, "I love you," and gave me a hug.

"Okay," I said. "Thanks."

I felt that she had heard information I hadn't, that she had some fears she was holding back, but that was alright. For now, I'd take the love and hugs.

After she left, I was alone for a while, and all I could do was look up at the ceiling and take a deep breath while a few tears ran down my cheeks. Only time would tell how fast I might recover. I knew I had to be in it for the long haul, but I had faith I could get better. Despite all my anxiety, I had this feeling that I might suddenly improve at any time.

On each of the last several days I woke up thinking, "Maybe this will be the day." Maybe it would be the day that I moved my toes or felt a tingling in my legs. I had the same optimism that Sam offered me in her words. It was a little shaky, but it was still optimism.

———————

I'm paralyzed. Literally paralyzed. I've been tackled and pinned to the ground a million times, so I thought I knew what it felt like to be trapped. I had no idea.

In the hospital bed I'm as motionless as a rock. My core—the abs and back muscles we use to twist, bend, straighten, and to do pretty much everything else—is a dead zone. My legs don't kick, push, or curl up anymore.

We talk about old people having one foot in the grave, but I feel like I have two legs in the grave, buried along with my torso. Only my head and shoulders and arms stick up through the earth, trying and failing to pull me out.

The optimism took a hit after I went to sleep. I must have woken up ten times during the night flooded with anxiety. I wanted to be walking in a month, but I couldn't even lift my hand to scratch my face. At four in the morning I just lay there and stared at the ceiling, listening to the heart rate monitor beep, beep, beep, while the dark room showed only silhouettes of the empty furniture.

Claustrophobia. The darkness felt like a heavy weight on top of me. I was afraid to leave home, but more than that I felt trapped by the sudden and complete stillness of my body. I have always been an active person. Now I was helplessly stuck in bed.

I couldn't roll over, sit up, or grab a cup of water. My arms were bent by the nurses so that my hands rested on my chest, like a guy in a coffin, and that's where they stayed, because I couldn't tell my triceps to straighten them out.

It really hit me. I was paralyzed. I had become a quadriplegic. I've been fighting this anxiety off and on ever since.

It was hard not to ask, "Why me?" or, "Why am I the one fighting this fight?" People crash their cars or knuckle their landings on the slopes every day. Why was I the one whose life had turned upside down?

Everyone, including me, seemed to want to believe that everything happens for a reason, but that seemed kind of insane.

I'd been saying my prayers when I could, even if they were a child's prayers sent up and out of the hospital room toward something I hoped could make all of this go away. My dad encouraged me to pray and brought me rosary beads, too. Sitting in my numb hand, though, they were pretty useless.

More importantly, Dad told me, as he had every night during childhood before the divorce, "You're good, you're strong, and you're smart. Say your prayers." It was so nice to hear it again, partly because it gave me some comfort in an uncomfortable situation, and partly because it was a reminder that through all the bullshit that divorce brings, he was still there.

In the dark of my room with my nerves on fire, I found myself turning to sports to calm myself. I know I sound like a sports nut sometimes, and I guess I am. But not in the way you might think. People think that because I was the varsity quarterback and a good team athlete that I'm a natural extrovert who enjoyed the public life. But I've always been an introvert, someone who feels most at home on my own or with a good friend or two. Sports were the best way for me to comfortably navigate social situations, because in sports everyone is active and goal oriented. There's no mystery about what to say or do.

Really I just think of myself as an ordinary kid who happened to love sports.

I'm so sports-focused that despite crushing my C6 vertebra a few days earlier, I was excited to watch the X Games from my Boston hospital bed. You'd think snowboarding would be the last thing I wanted to see, but I've been turning to sports my whole life to burn off the fire inside me and to show the world who I am through my actions.

I thought about the hours spent on the football field with some of my best friends. I thought about the bus rides home from games after a big win. Specifically, I thought about key games that we could have lost but in the end, we came out on top. For me, the best medicine is thinking about the toughest wins.

So I ignored the beep of the heart monitor and instead heard the referee's whistle as my mind drifted back to the two best games of the last football season. I was the Tyngsboro quarterback, and I was working my butt off to take our undefeated team to the finals. I was also hoping to get the attention of some college teams. I had even put a highlight reel online for the scouts to see.

Ironically, now it was me looking at the highlight reel in my mind.

First up was the game in Gardner. This was the true test of our team that season. We were undefeated, but Gardner was just as good as we were. The matchup was so even that whoever had final possession would probably win the game. Our team was clicking together perfectly, but Gardner had targeted our star running back, Chuckie Keenan, and so I was forced to throw all game long. I set a personal best for yards thrown, and luckily most of the throws were going to my tight end, Tom Lafferty, who caught everything. If he had to perform acrobatics to get the ball, he did it.

It was the end of the game, and we were up by only a few points. With a minute left in the fourth quarter, Gardner drove down the field to our ten-yard line. Their quarterback scrambled out of the pocket and threw a pass just over the fingertips of our defensive back for the touchdown.

With forty-four seconds left to keep our undefeated season alive, we were down by five. Gardner kicked off. Chuckie and I were the return men. I prayed the ball would go to Chuckie, but it came straight to me, and I did my best to give us good field position. I saw a gap in the middle of the field and took it sprinting as fast as I could. I dodged one tackle but was brought down at our own forty-five-yard line. Not bad field position, and we had a few tricks up our sleeve.

Our first play was a hook and ladder in which I threw a slant-and-sit pass to Tom, who pitched it back to Chuckie coming out of the backfield. The defense took the bait and swarmed Tom while Chuckie ran right by them for twenty-three yards.

Twenty-five seconds left with thirty-two yards to go. I checked in with the coach, and he called the play: Green Right Utah. Three receivers lined up on the right side going deep, and I took the snap from the shotgun and backed into a three-step drop with my eyes downfield, looking long. I had to dodge a defender coming in fast and almost fell down as I stepped back and to my right. Then, suddenly, there was Tom way downfield looking back at me. I took my chances and rifled the ball straight at him. He caught it in his chest and was smothered by Gardner, but it was too late. He had crossed the line into their end zone.

I went crazy. The team went crazy. But the game wasn't over. We tried for the two-point conversion instead of an extra point kick so that if Gardner got a field goal in the final seconds, they could only tie us, not win. But we came up short, inches short. So now we had to stop them cold. Our kicker sent down a nice dribbler that Gardner's return man had trouble handling, and we got down there before he found open space. They were trapped on their thirty-yard line with enough time for one play, maybe two.

Just one, as it turned out, since we set up a dime defense, with me in there as an extra defensive back. It was the only time I played defense all year, and I'm so happy I was in for that play. It worked beautifully. Tom rushed around the edge and sacked the quarterback, running the clock down to zero.

I had spent so much of my childhood in the backyard imagining a game like this, playing out the last-minute heroics with my friends. Now here it was, the delirious happiness of a kid's dream come true, one of the best experiences of my life.

Two weeks later we fought an even tougher battle. We arrived in Lunenberg in the dark on a rainy October night. The rain poured down onto the mud that a few hours before had been their nice baseball field. In the pregame warm-up I couldn't control the slippery ball and kept hoping to God that they'd cancel the game.

But we started what would be a long, hard slog with no passing, just a grind of running play after running play after running play with minimal gains. The teams were evenly matched, and we were evenly covered in mud. We entered the locker room at halftime with only fifty total yards on offense and a 0–0 tie.

The locker room was quiet. We sat there, soaked and tired, waiting for the third quarter and hoping the rain would let up.

Out we went. The rain fell harder, the slog was tougher, and time passed more slowly. The end of the game seemed so far away.

Then near the end of the third quarter we were making a solid drive, inching our way toward their end zone, Chuckie leading the charge. We made first and goal, and then we were in for six with Chuckie running it right up the middle. We were afraid to try a field goal in such slippery conditions, so we tried to convert for two but failed.

That woke Lunenberg up. As soon as they had possession, they marched down the field and answered our six points with six of their own. Like us, they failed to convert. We went into the fourth quarter tied, but neither side scored again. And so, the game that no one wanted to go into overtime went into overtime.

The good news was that according to high school football rules each possession began on the ten-yard line. We wouldn't have to slog the length of the field each time. Each team would get at least one possession. We won the coin toss but decided to give them the ball first. The plan was to make a big stop on defense and then try to score.

Sure enough, on the first play their quarterback scrambled out, and our defensive tackle stripped the ball out of his hand and fell on it. It was our ball now!

Now it was our turn on the ten-yard line. Any score now would win the game.

We tried a run up the middle but gained only a couple yards.

Then I tried a quarterback trick. I noticed they were trying to jump the snap count (i.e., predict when the ball was snapped to rush in a bit faster). So, I called a hard count, which is when a quarterback teases out the count until some impatient lineman comes offside. The penalty got us halfway to the goal. Just four yards to go.

A minute later I was rolling out to my left looking for a receiver in the end zone when I saw a small gap in the defense. I tucked the ball under my arm and went for it. I got tackled, but not before crossing the line to win the game!

Once again it was excitement and adrenaline and pride and joy all wrapped up in a moment that will stay with me forever. The pressure to win was off my shoulders, and we could collapse on the bus with our muddy uniforms as a badge of honor. We were still the undefeated pride of Tyngsboro.

Three months later I was a defeated mannequin in the snow.

Nothing can replace these memories and reliving them in that Boston hospital bed took my mind off not being able to move. For me, they're not only a comforting distraction that brings a smile to my face, they're a memory of what it means to keep the faith. I'm a fighter, even when I'm scared or anxious. That's what fighting means. To keep going even when the situation is hard. Feel the fear, as Dad says, but do it anyway.

But, to be honest, it's so much easier to say it than to do it. But I have to. I have to. And my memories are my allies in the fight.

I think everybody can relate to lying awake in the dark after a bad day and reminiscing about better times. Thinking about football was my version, but it was reminiscing with a purpose: to give me hope.

For some people, I think, hope is what they do when they don't have the energy or motivation to get something done. And, at times, some things are so far out of our control that hope is all we have. But for me, hope is what I use to get motivated, to take action. It's what keeps me focused.

I firmly believe that big things come to those who work for them. If I was going to get better, I needed to take it one day at a time and try to win each day.

But it would take time. How much time? No one knew, especially me. Weirdly, time was suddenly something I had too much of. Trapped in bed, trapped in my body, unable to burn time by running, jumping, playing as I always had, I was floating in a stagnant pool of time. During a dark night like this one, time was everywhere around me, so quiet and still that it felt nonexistent. Looking into the past to imagine the future was all I had.

Hours before my flight to Atlanta, I lay there in silence with fear, hope, anxiety, and anticipation hitting me in waves. My thoughts were all questions: *What is the hospital like? Will I walk out of it? How do I bounce back if I can't bounce?* Nobody could give me answers, and so it was on me to do whatever I could to make it happen.

Finally, I managed to get a few hours of sleep. Then things started to happen. Doctors stopped by for their final visit, and the nurses came in to give me some medication and prepare my IV lines for transport to Hanscom Air Force Base in Bedford, Massachusetts.

Moments before the EMTs placed me on the stretcher, my mom took a picture of me in the hospital bed. I looked cheerful and anxious and helpless and hopeful. A week after my accident, I thought that I had been on a hell of a ride already, but really I was just at the beginning of my life's journey.

4

THE ADJUSTMENTS

My eyes are open, but I can't see. I can't hear. I think I'm passing out. Everything is fading to black.

Why is this happening again? Why now?

But I'm not lying in the snow looking up at beautiful flakes floating down around me. I'm in a small white room with nurses and my mom staring at me as I sink into myself.

All I want to do is sit up. Is that so much to ask?

Why do I keep forgetting to say the obvious—that my parents were incredibly loving and supportive through all of this? I guess I'm still young enough that I live in my head. I'm definitely too young to know how hard an adjustment like this was for my parents, or for any parents. I mean, I can see how Mom and Dad turned their lives upside down to help me, but for me to get into their heads is still a challenge. You raise a kid for sixteen years, putting all your love and advice and hopes into them, and then *Bam!*, the kid tries a frontside rodeo and all hell breaks loose. What is that really like for them?

One thing I do know. I could always look to Mom and Dad for an example of the strength and patience I needed to get through this. It was true before the accident, and it was true now. Mom was my anchor, always there when I needed her, and Dad was my role model. We'd all been through hard times once already.

My parents divorced when I was ten. It was tough but not a nightmare. I was in fifth grade, not mature enough to deal with the fallout. Sam was older and saw more, felt more. I didn't see it coming, and to be honest there were nights early on that I cried about it. Family matters to me. Plus, none of my friends had divorced parents so it was tougher to navigate when I didn't have anything to reference.

For the first ten years of my life, I had both parents home every day, then suddenly it was only my mom coming back after work. My dad did everything he could to stay connected. I spent every other weekend with him, and he and I ate dinner at a local sandwich shop once a week. But mainly Dad coached nearly every team that I played on. From baseball to football to wrestling he was always there. And since sports filled up most of my week, that meant I saw him constantly.

Better yet, sports were the thing that got my parents in the same place at the same time. For the length of a game, sports paused the reality of divorce. I was worried about reading a defense rather than reading the look on my parents' faces.

Eventually, the separation boosted my independence and made me grow up a little faster. I learned as I went, as did Sam and our parents. The main things I learned from Mom and Dad to deal with hard times were (1) show unconditional love and (2) work hard to make things better.

Which is what they were doing on that Saturday morning of my departure. My parents packed up everything I needed, and then Dad said he loved me and would see me in Atlanta in two weeks. Mom and I headed to Hanscom airfield.

The adventure of traveling to Atlanta quickly became just another nasty ambulance ride. The stench of cleaning chemicals and the bumpy roads made me sick the whole way to Hanscom. The crew gave me a valium, and I don't remember much except for one thing: Massachusetts was still very cold. Going to Atlanta was scary, but at least I could look forward to warm weather.

We arrived at Hanscom to see a tiny, ten-seat Lear jet they were calling an "Air Ambulance." Uh oh. I was glad to be doped up. I wasn't really excited to add air sickness to my extensive ambulance experience.

I passed out and woke groggily when we touched down at Hartsfield-Jackson Airport in Atlanta. I really have no memory of the flight and oddly have never even asked my mother what it was like. I know she was really worried about transporting me and my injured neck so far.

But now we had safely landed in balmy Atlanta. They opened the door.

Wait, what? It was still cold. I had a northerner's fantasy of the South and dreamed it would be lovely with warm tropical breezes, but at best it was ten degrees warmer than Boston.

What's the point of living in the South if you need AC all summer and heat all winter?

And the city. Ugh. I'm a small-town kid. I've lived in Tyngsboro my entire life. It's a town in the woods of northern Massachusetts, just below the New Hampshire border. Atlanta was huge and strange to me. I don't like traffic, I don't like city noises, and I don't like a world made of concrete. I mean, some concrete is okay, but I'm outdoors a lot and need trees and open green spaces. I know I had bigger worries than my setting, but with everything being so different and weird, the view wasn't putting me at ease.

Maybe my first impressions of my new home were a little tainted by the vomiting, though. The valium had worn off, and the ride to the Shepherd Center wasn't any prettier on the inside of the ambulance than it was on the outside.

As they wheeled me into the building, I looked up and saw butterflies painted on the ceiling tiles. Back in Lowell I had hoped for something nicer than just industrial lighting and Trauma signs, but now I wasn't so sure. Was I in a rehabilitation hospital or an asylum?

Finally Mom and I settled into Room 430. It was simple and small with off-white walls, containing a hospital bed, a chair, a TV, a desk, and a bit of closet space. And a window, but a window with a view of a concrete wall and other patients' windows. If I got real close to the glass and looked to the left, I could see a concrete walkway leading to four-lane Peachtree Road and its constant traffic. So much for inspiration from nature to help with my recovery.

I was farther down the rabbit hole and nothing looked like home. *Oh well*, I thought, *it's only another hurdle*. I would have to keep a smile on my face and find inspiration elsewhere.

And I was wanting a little inspiration right then. Lying in a new bed, I felt the strange weight of this place and what I'd just done. I rarely ever left home, but now I'd traveled down the east coast to a hospital that might get me back on my feet. Or not.

The Shepherd Center staff didn't waste any time. A few hours after my arrival they showed up in my room to give me my first task: to sit up for the first time in nine days. The last time I tried to sit up was while lying in the snow after the fall. That was a terrible idea. But now, post-surgery and surrounded by experts, sitting up would be simple, right?

Wrong. My body clearly wasn't expecting it, and in a few seconds everything went to hell. Lightheaded and dizzy, I quickly sank toward unconsciousness. My hearing cut out. My vision faded to black. I had no idea what was going on, but it felt like my brain's battery had failed without warning.

I was panicking and blacking out at the same time. This was different than the shock and hypothermia I'd felt in Eric's yard. This was some kind of system failure. Worse, the shock of it made it hard for me to explain what was going on. But they eased me back down, and I slowly recovered.

My blood pressure was in the basement. Normal pressure for most people is 120/80. It had always been lower for me, though, because I'm an athlete (increase in exercise and stamina lowers blood pressure). Now my numbers had fallen off a cliff to 60/40. It's like I was hibernating. All I could do was stay down and have them put my feet up.

Sunday we tried again, with the same result. They were fitting me for a wheelchair but the fact that I couldn't sit up straight without passing out made that pretty complicated.

It didn't help that I'd been losing weight like an hourglass loses sand. I was pretty lean to begin with, but I was dropping about a pound per day, with ten pounds gone since the accident. This was a hell of a weight-loss plan, but I didn't need it and I can't recommend it.

Right out of the gate this blood pressure thing upset all my rehabilitation plans. If I couldn't sit up, then how could I exercise?

Dr. Murray led my medical team. He was in charge of the Shepherd Center's spinal cord center for adolescents, and he dealt with hundreds of spinal injuries a year, but even he couldn't get a handle on my blood pressure. He started me on one medication, then another, then another, each proven to raise blood pressure. Nothing worked. I tried maximum doses of Midodrine and Florinef but sitting up was still like climbing Mt. Everest without oxygen. Dr. Murray soon experimented with medications for other illnesses that had a known side effect of raising blood pressure: Buspar (for anxiety), Neurontin (for nerve pain), and even salt tablets (to retain water). It all helped but wasn't enough.

As a side note, I felt like I needed medication to understand Dr. Murray's accent. He was obviously a son of the Deep South, and his accent kind of threw me sometimes. It was "y'all" this and "y'all" that. For a born-and-raised Boston kid, it was a foreign language. But it was a language I'd have to learn, because Dr. Murray was the expert working to turn my life around.

Which was good, because things got worse on that first weekend. Like some kind of cosmic joke, pretty much as soon as I got to Atlanta, I started getting cold. Like shivering-all-the-time kind of cold. We cranked the thermostat in my room to seventy degrees, and I was still begging the nurses to bring me heated blankets. Low body temperature is a common side effect for SCIs (spinal cord injuries), and now it had found me.

At least for my mom, who was sharing my room, Atlanta was now hot and balmy.

Come Monday, shivering or not, lightheaded or not, it was time to start working on getting better. But preparing for my day took over an hour. First thing was to swallow a small mountain of blood pressure pills. I've never liked taking pills, and now it was ten times worse. I was still wearing the huge cervical collar, and I didn't have the arm or hand coordination to take them by myself. A nurse placed them in my mouth as carefully as she could, but sometimes they got stuck in my throat. Choking on pills when I couldn't move really sucked.

Once the pills were down, I'd lay back for a few minutes, hoping the blood pressure medication would kick in to stabilize me for the day. More often than not this didn't happen, and each day was a struggle. It's hard to do anything when you're fighting the urge to faint.

Then I had to get dressed. Or, I had to *be* dressed. My arms and hands were useless, my torso and lower body were dead to me, so I needed 100 percent assistance. All I could do was lie there and watch a nurse put my pants on, pull a T-shirt over my head, and slip on my socks and shoes. I felt like a mannequin again.

Twenty minutes of stretching came next. This was to prevent spasms in the muscles that were atrophying and freaking out because they couldn't talk to the brain. Nurses did the stretching for me, of course. I wanted to help with my legs, so the staff hooked my arms through a tether looped over my foot, and I'd pull as best I could. Which wasn't much at all.

By this point I was more than ready for breakfast, but my stomach was the only part of me that enjoyed it. Nothing was more depressing than having my mother or father spoon-feed me my morning meal. I felt like a baby in a high chair. But this baby needed to eat to gain weight and help elevate his blood pressure, so I wolfed down every bite.

Then I had to be shifted out of bed into a wheelchair. The

transfer was done with a Hoyer lift—a small crane attached to the ceiling and hooked to four loops on a net placed beneath me. I was lifted up, moved over the side of the bed, and lowered into the chair.

Suspended like a fish in a net, I knew this wasn't the life I wanted. I wanted freedom; I wanted mobility. Seeing how much equipment and effort was needed to get me out of bed made me want to cry. I wasn't sure what my recovery would look like but getting free of this contraption had to be part of it.

The last thing on the morning to-do list was to have my teeth brushed. You can understand how I felt about this by imagining that suddenly your mom is your dentist, and that you'll have to go to the dentist every morning for the rest of your life.

And so, an hour after waking, I was dizzy, shivering, frustrated, and a little sad, but ready to start the day. I could sense a battle forming between two forces: my desire for independence and my lack of patience. I was fighting to get my life back, but I had to fight slowly.

Insanely slowly.

In a new life full of adjustments, I think my biggest adjustment was allowing for the time required to do any stupid little thing. Everything took time, and I hated it. Even the simplest tasks took much longer than I thought they should. Suddenly my biggest goals weren't walking and playing football with my friends. They were feeding myself and getting out of bed on my own.

I was used to being a normal teenager and doing everyday tasks at the last minute and in a hurry. Here in Atlanta, all the slow, fussy preparation was testing my patience every hour of every day.

I just wanted things to go back to normal. Part of me was still in denial. I hadn't fully accepted my injury. Patience was something I was going to have to learn. But not the kind of three-second patience that a good quarterback uses to wait for the right receiver. I had to learn the three-month or, Lord forbid, the three-year or three-decade patience of a guy with a serious spinal injury. This was going to take some serious willpower.

So the long morning routines were a rough start, but they were good training for the long road ahead.

———————

I do not want to spend my life in this public cage, where everyone can see how weak and helpless I am. A power wheelchair is an amazing technical gift—I can't imagine what life was like for SCI patients fifty or a hundred years ago—but I love my body and all I've been able to do with it in sports, and I don't want it to end up a puppet flopped down into a golf cart.

As an athlete since childhood, I exercised constantly and strived to be the best I could be. I was familiar with discipline and hard work. So hypothetically, rehabilitation wasn't any different. My job was to set tasks and accomplish them as best I could.

But I felt like a guitarist who had been kidnapped from civilization and sent into the rainforest to cut down a tree and make a guitar from it. I wasn't training my body so much as I was reinventing my life from scratch.

And the most obvious change to my life was a bulky three-hundred-pound wheelchair powered by a battery and steered by a joystick. It didn't take me long to (a) find the button that cranked up the speed of the chair and (b) figure out why they hadn't told me how to do it. At full speed—a blazing seven miles per hour—if I slammed into a doorway or chair, I did it with about five hundred pounds of force. This somehow got the attention of nurses, therapists, custodians, parents, visitors, and doctors, all of whom told me to slow down. I heard them, but I thought a better solution was to maintain speed and figure out how to steer better, so that's what I did. I figured it wasn't serious disobedience if I learned quickly enough.

Finally, on Monday morning, I drove my demolition car to a meeting with my rehabilitation team. It did not start well. My case managers told me I would stay at least eight weeks because of my weak condition. I was losing a pound per day, my muscles were shriveling, I was shivering, and my blood pressure was tenuous at best. After eight weeks they would decide if I needed to stay longer.

Parked in my chair, tilted back so as to not pass out, a rush of sadness came over me. It had been a week and a half since the accident, and other than still being alive I had yet to receive any serious good news at all. Really I was struggling just to get to the starting line.

At least my daily rehab schedule, now that it was on paper, was simple enough. After the epic saga of getting out of bed, I had an hour and a half session of either physical therapy (PT) or occupational therapy (OT), followed by strength training. Every afternoon, same thing, with the occasional addition of some recreational therapy. I had some injury education classes to attend a few times per week to help me understand what had happened to my body and what to expect long-term. On Saturdays, I had one session of either PT or OT, alternating week to week.

I was impressed with the therapy gym. Other than my room, that's where I'd spend all my time. It was a wide-open room with ten therapy mats spread around it, each two feet off the floor and about the size of a queen bed. At any given time, two or three patients were on or around the mats, plus a few others working out on the FES (functional electrical stimulation) bikes lined up along windows looking out onto Peachtree Road. There were Hoyer lifts and stands for free weights, TheraBands, medicine balls, and other PT tools. Shepherd Center staff were everywhere. I was amazed at how many people were involved in our care.

What I didn't know was how steep the learning curve would be for each of my therapies.

And I didn't know who my therapists were and how well we'd get along.

First up was Patty Antcliff, occupational therapist. I liked her right away. Blonde, funny, bubbly, supportive, Patty was all about the tough love approach to therapy. More love than tough, though, so her message was "I love you, but I'm going to push you too!"

When she first described our goals, though, occupational therapy seemed really pointless. Why would I need to practice making a phone call, brushing my teeth, or taking a shower? I'd been doing those things my whole life, and once I got better I would do them as I always had.

Patty's job was to help me understand how to adapt to the changes in my body. But I didn't want to adapt to my new body. I wanted to rediscover my old one.

She reminded me that I had a complete C6 injury, with no motion or sensation from my chest down. (An "incomplete" injury is one that still allows some feeling or movement below the expected level of injury.) I could only move my head, shoulders, upper back, and biceps.

Patty taught me that occupational therapy is all about relearning how to live everyday life within the reality of your injury. It was about becoming independent again. While still hoping that I would miraculously get better, I could definitely understand the need for independence if things stayed the way they were. And so suddenly, what seemed unnecessary became essential.

And impossible. Without functioning triceps, wrists, or hands, how was I going to comb my hair or eat my lunch? How the hell would I ever put a shirt on? To start, Patty set me up with a universal cuff for each hand so I could brush my teeth and eat. The cuff wrapped around the middle of my hand and had little sleeves for a toothbrush or utensil. At first, I could only flail around my mouth with the brush and stab clumsily at a bite of food to try to get it into my mouth. My teeth didn't get super clean, and most of my food fell off the fork on the way up.

Everything was so hard in those first sessions with Patty. After each session, I went back to my room feeling pretty depressed. Mom was waiting there, worried about me and asking lots of questions, many of which I really didn't want to answer. She knew when to give me space, though, and when to make a joke or just show me some love. Lord knows I needed all of it.

Physical therapy with Cathi Dugger seemed a little more straightforward. As an athlete with a history of injuries I knew a bit more about the concept. But for Cathi, dark-haired and athletic with serious eyes, tough love was especially tough. She had a big smile, but right away I could tell that she was a no-nonsense kind of person and she was not going to let me get away with anything. She said she'd push me to my limit in order to show me what I was capable of.

The big obstacle, though, was that she was a Yankees fan. Even worse, she was *from* New York, so she was incurable. We had lots of friendly banter during our sessions. I of course mentioned the great Sox comeback in the ALCS in 2004, but she was quick to remind me of the million championships New York had won. And we had a date to get ready for: April 1, around the time I might be leaving Shepherd, when our teams met for the opening game of the season. Hopefully the Sox and I would both be in top shape when the day came.

In the meantime there was an overwhelming amount of PT to do, and Cathi worked me like I'd never been worked before. One of my first tasks was prop sitting, which is sitting upright with your hands braced behind you. Without any core muscles to hold me up, and without any triceps, I had to put my hands far enough back that I could lock my elbows and activate my shoulders instead of my useless triceps.

Not to put too fine a point on my weakness, but prop sitting is something a baby learns when it's first getting past the cute-lump-in-a-blanket stage. And this baby struggled. Again and again I threw my hands behind me, but without functioning triceps it was like pushing a rope. Cathi stood behind and spotted me as I failed repetition after repetition.

Strength training sessions were meant to get my power and muscle mass back, or at least as much of it as possible. My disconnected muscles were atrophying, and I'd hardly moved any part of my body since the accident. Plus I still had the metabolism of a teenage athlete. If I didn't eat well and work hard to rebuild the few good muscles that remained, I'd become the invisible man. Every day I saw in the mirror that my wrists and forearms were shrinking.

Our strategy was a long list of TheraBand exercises, each of which isolated individual muscles. Muscles I still had control over, that is. I couldn't exercise the ones that weren't listening to my brain.

Everything was brutally hard. During my early struggles with OT, PT, and strength training, I counted the minutes until each session was over. I was doing so much work for so little progress. I was dizzy from low blood pressure. Sometimes I was so tired after sessions that I'd tilt the chair back and immediately take a nap. Days felt like they would never end. Then at night I went to bed dreading having to wake up to do it all over again.

Finally, the easiest and hardest work I did was recreational therapy with Sarah Begeal. Every other Friday I was loaded up in a van with a few other adolescent SCI patients to go on an outing somewhere in Atlanta. Only a field trip, right? A breath of fresh air and a nice break from all the hard exercise, right?

Not so much. It was emotionally exhausting.

Our first trip—only a week after I arrived—was to the Lenox Square Mall down the road from the Shepherd Center. It seemed like a new world. I was in a power wheelchair controlled by a joystick. I still wore a huge plastic cervical neck brace. And I was seeing the world from four feet off the ground, rather than the five-foot-ten elevation I had spent my entire life to reach.

Five of us with spinal injuries ranging from C5 to L5—some in manual chairs and some, like me, in power chairs—rolled up together outside the front doors of the mall. I looked in and saw all the shoppers and thought, *There is no way I am going in there just so people can stare at me.* I had felt that way since the first moment Sarah described the program. I wanted to focus on my physical recovery instead.

Everyone at Shepherd told me it was important to practice getting back into the world, but I only went because it was a requirement of the rehab program. I didn't want to try new things or reenter society looking like this. The fear was building up fast. I knew people would gawk at me and wonder, *What happened to that kid?*

And that's pretty much how it went. Or so it seemed to me. Probably not too many people noticed or cared, but even an innocent glance from a passerby felt like a stare. Mostly young kids were the ones who couldn't take their eyes off us as we rolled by. I had to work so hard—therapy, right?—to ignore people and focus on what I wanted to see and do, but really the eyes of random strangers were all I could think about.

I never realized how much you can be looked at and judged based on whether or not you can walk. I had lived a sheltered, lucky life in my Boston suburb and never had to deal with being perceived as "different" in any way. I didn't know anyone stuck in a wheelchair.

I'm still me. I'm still the same person on the inside. I don't want sympathy. I want ordinary respect, the kind of respect that able-bodied people assume is the fabric that binds them all together. I don't want to be in a separate category merely because I'm in this stupid power chair looking up at you.

Yes, you have questions when you see me: What the hell happened to him? Can he get better? Is his brain as messed up as his body? But keep in mind, I don't wonder about your mental health when I see you wearing a Yankees hat or walking around with your zipper down.

I could have talked about all this with Cheryl Lindon, the counselor for the adolescent team. We met once a week, and I liked to stop by her office to say hi once in a while if the door was open. Cheryl was super friendly and encouraging, and it was easy to talk with her about my hobbies or life goals or how PT was going, that sort of stuff. But I didn't want to get into the heavy topics with her. The trip to the mall was embarrassing, and it opened up a whole fear of the future that I wanted to keep to myself.

So yes, this going out in public thing was a real challenge for me. I had a lot to figure out. I knew that the recreational therapy was important, just like I knew from my pathetic early failures in OT and PT that I wasn't going to waltz out of Atlanta in eight weeks, but I couldn't stand the way I looked (and was looked at) in the power chair.

That day in the mall I decided that I needed to get out of the power chair and into a manual one as fast as humanly possible. I had my basic life skills to sort out—brushing my teeth, feeding myself, sitting upright—but I desperately wanted to get into a manual chair.

Dr. Murray and the team were equally desperate to improve my blood pressure. Because the drugs were insufficient, Dr. Murray decided it was time to turn me into an Egyptian mummy. They put knee-high pressure socks on me to increase circulation and keep the blood from pooling in my legs. Still not enough. They added an Ace bandage over the socks to increase the tightness. Still not enough. Finally, they wrapped my entire midsection to reduce the movement of my diaphragm. All of this added a shrink-wrapping stage to my already long morning ritual.

The team was stunned that my blood pressure remained a problem after all these interventions, but through their hard work and experimentation they finally got me to a point where I could sit tilted upward (though not quite upright) in the hospital bed or wheelchair. A week after arrival, I still felt lightheaded, but it was progress.

Attitude was everything. And so, there was one rule that Cathi and Patty shared. I was not allowed to use the words *I can't*. In the early days so many things seemed impossible to me. I knew that I'd never be able to do them. *I can't* seemed like the perfect words for the situation. The problem was that Cathi and Patty knew better, and they decided to do something about it.

The rule was that every time I said it, I had to buy them a Diet Coke. Cathi was especially tough about this. I was careful but did end up making a few long trips from the fourth-floor gym down to the soda machine in the first-floor lobby. I trusted them enough to make a good effort before feeling like a failure. And as time went on, I realized things got a bit easier as I practiced. Not easy, but easier.

5

AND SO IT BEGINS

Aliens are trying to hatch out of my body.

My abs just tightened into a death knot, then released. A minute ago my legs scissored randomly. Now my quads are trembling like I stuck my toes in a socket. The bed is shaking.

I'm not moving these muscles. The nerves are issuing their own orders now that they've been without a central command for a few weeks. But it's like watching five-year-olds play soccer for the first time. No rules, no goals, only random muscle movement.

The twitching isn't voluntary, but "involuntary" sounds like they're controlled by someone else.

At my next PT session with Cathi I asked if I could try out a manual chair. I'm sure she knew it was too early, but like all Shepherd staff she totally supported anything I wanted to try.

Cathi was a competitive athlete herself, so she knew where I was coming from. She fetched the chair from downstairs, and when I saw it rolling down the hallway, I got really excited. She plunked me down into it with the Hoyer lift, and I sat there for a few minutes like a middle-aged guy fantasizing behind the wheel of a 911 Cayenne at a Porsche dealership. It was lighter and smaller and . . . not a damn golf cart. I felt free just sitting in it.

Now for a test drive. I put my palms on the push rims (the outer edge of the wheel) but they slid off the plastic. Cathi found push rims with a rubber coating that I could get a little bit of a grip on, which helped a little, but I still slipped off. Then she gave me sticky gloves that I could use on the rubber coated rims. Finally, I had total friction. Let's go!

Wait, are the wheels locked? Who's holding me back? I really thought someone had grabbed the handles of the chair. I had no arm strength, and I definitely didn't have any grip strength. I pushed until my palms turned red and my fingers became useless.

Sisyphus couldn't budge his stone. And it wasn't even uphill! At best I moved the chair two or three feet. How could that be? I saw other SCI patients cruising around all the time.

I was really disappointed, but I had a choice. I could see only the failure, or I could use it as motivation.

So I asked Cathi if I could keep the chair in my room. I wanted it for practice, and I wanted the reminder of the life I wanted to live once I left Shepherd.

I could hear my dad talking through me when I asked Cathi to leave the chair. He had always been my life coach. "Don't be lazy!" Check. "Take it one day at a time." Check. "Give it your best shot and don't be afraid to get your ass kicked." Check and check.

But it was brutally hard to keep his voice and message clear in my head. Through these first few weeks my motivation level was up and down like a roller coaster. My work ethic and optimism pushed me forward, but bad news and failures set me back. Downhill and uphill, uphill and downhill.

Alone at night, hour after hour, I tried to use sheer will to make my muscles work. I fixed my eyes on my hands or wrists or triceps and said, *Move!* inside my head over and over.

Well, to be honest, what I said was harsher than that—more like, *Fucking move!*—especially as the constant failure made me feel like shit. Sometimes if I was a little too intense, I actually muttered the curse words out loud. I probably sounded a little crazy talking to myself, but I was on a mission.

I desperately wanted to move my hands. They were the center of my sports universe. But my fingers felt like they were wrapped in rubber bands. There was phantom sensation there—it felt like my fingers were moving—but nothing I cursed or mumbled or imagined made a real difference.

Then I remembered the last time my hands were numb. At the time of my accident, I was working in the back of the Flint's Corner Pizza place, which was just down the road from our house. It was winter, and I had to take the freezer shelves outside once a week to hose and scrub them down. It took half an hour, and I could barely feel my hands by the end of it. I hated that chore and was always wondering how I could avoid it. Now, just a few months later, paralyzed Jack would do anything to change positions with cleaning Jack.

It occurred to me that Dad might be having some of that pizza for dinner at that very moment, since he was managing the renovation of Mom's house every night after work.

Two weeks after I got to Atlanta Dad finally took a break to visit. It was around the time I failed in the manual chair, and I was feeling pretty overwhelmed. Weak and lightheaded, wearing the collar and stuck helplessly every day in either the power chair or a hospital bed, I was definitely getting my ass kicked. And now here was Dad, so familiar and so important, smiling at me in my room. He came right alongside the bed and gave me a hug, then looked me in the eye. He didn't say a word at first, but I could see he was tearing up a bit.

At first all I could do was stare at him. I knew I had really missed him, but I didn't realize how much until the dam broke. I tried to hold it together but couldn't.

Crying in front of a dad who loves you isn't the worst thing, though it's not easy. But not being able to wipe your own runny nose and eyes just adds insult to injury. Literally.

We had the whole weekend together, the first of his twice-a-month visits he'd do while I was in Atlanta. It was nice to show him around the hospital, take him out to hang in the courtyard, and generally reconnect with him. Even having him feed me in the morning—as embarrassing as it was—felt good. I needed the boost that only he could give me.

And I could feel how much he wanted me to get better. Dad wanted it just as badly as I did, and kept telling me to keep my spirits up, to work hard, and to wait for the good stuff to happen.

At one point that weekend Dad saw my leg shaking a little bit, and I had to tell him that spasticity had increased and was making all sorts of weird stuff happen. My legs and abs and hands randomly clenched and shook.

Not a good time to be holding a knife or a baby.

Before, I'd had some occasional spasming at night in bed, but all the exercising had kept the muscles too fatigued to really act up. Until now. Now they were getting busy.

Mostly this happened when I was lying down, but I dealt with it in the chair too. Sometimes the spasms were big enough that they looked like a seizure. They weren't painful, only annoying.

The staff had warned us that the spasming would get worse and might stay with me forever. So I was kind of ready, but probably about as ready as a space tourist having their first experience of weightlessness. It was definitely bizarre, but it wasn't scary, because it was kind of cool to see my body hijacked like this. The contracting muscles were like Frankenstein's monster. They belonged to me but were beyond my control.

As with so much in my new life, all I could really say for sure was, "This happens now."

I kept hoping that the spasms meant that some neurological function was returning, but I had to face the truth. My nerves were firing randomly not rebuilding connections through my spine to my brain.

I learned a lot of this from Dr. Murray, who made a point of teaching me about what was going on with my spine and body. He showed me X-rays and other images of my spinal injury, and every time he made his rounds he talked to me about all the changes, good and bad, that were happening. I could hear the cart rolling down the hallway as he made his rounds, and the sound filled me with anxiety and hope. I hoped that he would give me some good news about my injury, and I was anxious that he wouldn't.

One of the things he taught me was that the neurology of spinal injuries is too complicated to fully predict the results. Each injury is a like a bomb hitting a library. Sure, you know the basic cause and effect, but you won't really know what information is still readable until the rubble is cleared.

Dr. Murray also talked to me about starting a family. That is, he reassured me that when I got older, whether I started walking again or not, I could have kids. There's a stereotype out there that if you're in a wheelchair, you can't have a child naturally, but it's just plain wrong. They taught us in our injury education classes that different SCIs affected sexual function differently. Typically, unless you damage the lower back (the upper sacral and lower lumbar vertebrae, specifically), you'll probably have decent sexual function. What's kind of funny is that, neurologically, some sexual function is fairly independent from the brain. But we already knew that.

Anyway, the basic truth was yes, many SCI patients could have kids the old-fashioned way. I was a junior in high school, so being a dad wasn't really on my radar. Still, I was glad not to have to worry about it. I had enough things to worry about.

I was grateful that the other kids in the program understood what I was going through. We were always supporting each other in the gym, giving compliments when someone hit a new recovery landmark. One guy I spent time with was Taylor, also from Massachusetts, and together we were known as the "Boston Boys." Taylor had skied into a tree and was now in a manual chair dealing with a thoracic injury. He had more function than I did, so while I was trying to get a shirt on, he was climbing from the floor into his chair. It was cool seeing him accomplish that.

And there was Corey, from Florida, who lived right next to me in Room 429. His lumbar injury came from another typical teen SCI situation. He was one of three kids not wearing seatbelts in a pickup that rolled over. Corey had been thrown into a tree, but he was lucky compared to the friend who died at the scene.

What I appreciated about Corey was that he was as serious as

I was about getting better, which meant that sometimes we both would get pissed when another patient wasn't taking rehab seriously or was too busy feeling sorry for himself. Like the kid with a relatively minor incomplete injury who refused to play when a group of us were hitting a balloon around as a fun way to work on dexterity. He was in the circle, and the balloon came down to his feet, but he looked at it and then looked away.

It irked Corey and me that the kid didn't get it. He had really good voluntary movement in his legs and decent prospects if he put the work in, but he sat there sulking as people with much more serious injuries made the effort. The rest of us would have killed to have his level of function, but this kid didn't care. We understood his pain but not his response to it.

We all shared a bond based on our injuries, but we also knew that we were there for a short time, with different schedules and individualized goals. And because everything we were going through was still pretty new and raw, on some level each of us still felt isolated. It's like we were prisoners of war together, helping each other when we could but mostly worrying about going home.

One way the program connected us was through an ongoing gift exchange. When someone graduated they passed on an object given to them by a previous patient. Each graduate signed it before passing it along to someone they liked or who was improving or who needed a little boost, and they wished the recipient good luck with their recovery. I had already received a basketball and a wooden block. The objects didn't matter, but it was a nice way of remembering that we weren't alone in the fight and that before long we would graduate too.

I also had Cheryl to talk to. She had this tiny office—a closet, really—with a small table and desk lamp, but we rarely spent time there. Cheryl asked where I wanted to go, and we'd stroll (and roll) through the hospital talking together. She was great at conversation and did most of the talking, but she always got me to tell her something about myself. Cheryl understood I was competitive and motivated and that I wasn't big on talking about my feelings. She never directly asked how I felt about the injury or my medical prognosis. She didn't ask about my fears.

Her style was to keep it informal but still motivate me to be positive. When I said I wasn't sure about going to college anymore, she helped me see that it was still a real possibility. When I was feeling weak, she noted the improvements the other therapists had told her I'd made and said, "I didn't know you were that strong already." She was more of a friend than a therapist, it seemed, and she knew how to give me a good boost.

I should mention another good friend, someone I got along with so well that I even let him lie on my bed during the day when I was in my chair. He was pretty chill. In fact, Frosty was professionally chill. His job was to relax everyone he met, since he was a therapy dog who belonged to Rebecca, one of the SCI unit's nurses. Frosty was a big yellow lab who spent much of his day in Rebecca's office, so he was happy whenever my mom stopped by to borrow him. Sometimes all I had to do was look at Mom with raised eyebrows and a sad face, and she'd laugh before getting up and walking across the hall to get the dog. When the weather was nice, we'd walk him outside in the courtyard.

But walking Frosty wasn't going to get me in better shape. I was struggling to make some gains before Derek and Justin arrived. I was anxious about them seeing me so weak and helpless, and still stuck in the power chair. The problem was that most days when I got back from therapy, I could barely lift my arms, never mind push my body weight around. So the manual chair didn't see much activity, even though Cathi and I tried a couple more tricks to get me moving. She found a knobbed push rim, which looked a little like an old-fashioned ship's wheel. It was much easier to push on those small, padded spokes, but I still wasn't strong enough.

Not that a power chair didn't have advantages. I really needed the tilt function on the power chair when my blood pressure dropped, as it so often did. And then there was the recreational therapy trip to Kennesaw State University when everybody but me was in manual chairs. We were assessing the campus for accessibility, and it was a big place with some hills. So when things got tough, the other kids lined up single file behind me like train cars, holding onto each other as the first one held onto my chair. We chugged along like that long enough that I started to wonder if they only brought me along for my motor. Maybe I should have charged Uber rates.

I had other adventures with the power chair too. The first time I left the Shepherd Center without hospital staff was when I went to get my hair cut. My mom and I only had to go a quarter mile down Peachtree Road, which is really busy, but I didn't want to use the sidewalk. The chair takes up too much space if there are pedestrians, and there's nowhere to go if an obstacle comes up. So, I cruised down the edge of Peachtree like a cyclist, with my mom walking next to me on the sidewalk. I had to swerve into the road a bit to get around some construction, but we made it to the barber and back without a problem.

When I told my therapists about it, though, they freaked out. Peachtree is one of downtown Atlanta's busiest roads, with a 35-mph speed limit that few people obeyed. All sorts of high-end sports cars that you don't often see in Massachusetts—because

Atlanta doesn't have snow, sand, and salt to deal with—were zipping by at 50 mph. I could hear the V10 engines coming from a mile away but didn't worry about it. I figured that a guy in a neck brace and power chair wouldn't be too hard to see. But I'll admit I would have been toast if someone was distracted by their phone and plowed into me.

I understood the concern, but I needed to live my life, even if I didn't have my previous mobility and strength. This is what people mean when they talk about the "dignity of risk." People in wheelchairs, people with special needs, and the elderly all need additional levels of assistance but that doesn't mean they shouldn't be allowed to live as fully as possible.

It was really hard to admit I was in one of those categories, but I couldn't argue with it. A month earlier I was a healthy kid with a strong upper body. Now my arms burned out if I lifted my hands to my face more than a few times per day. My left arm was pretty much dead weight. I actually had to strap it to the armrest to keep it from falling off when I bumped into things.

My right arm was improving faster because I was right-hand dominant, but it still couldn't hold weight or reach to grab things. I needed a bit of assistance, something that kept my arm from fatiguing during the hard work of therapy while still allowing me to build strength. I figured there had to be something like that, so I asked Patty.

Lucky for me, Patty had an answer for everything. She dug around in a closet and found a mobile arm support. It's a simple mechanical arm that attached directly to the back of my chair. It consisted of a few metal rods, a cuff that attached to my arm and hand, and rubber bands to help fight against gravity. Bent at a 90-degree angle, the rubber bands suspended the rods and stretched like a muscle when I reached downward and contracted when I brought my arm up.

The mobile arm support didn't bring me back to pre-injury mobility, but it increased my capacity tenfold. Patty and I were able to push harder in therapy and add variations for learning daily tasks. My range of motion was improved so much that I could reach up over my head and stretch shoulder muscles for the first time. I could even play a few games on my phone, which was one of the little things that made life feel a bit more normal.

Best of all, I could fulfill my promise to respond to the hundreds of messages that had started coming my way back in Boston. I said I'd do it as soon as I was able, and now I was able. The long hours sitting in my room at the Shepherd Center took on new life. I strapped a stylus onto my hand and ever so slowly typed out each note. It was a Sisyphean task, because I was obsessed with responding to every message even as more arrived each day. I was so slow at typing that I had to get right to the point. These people had taken time out of their lives to send me a message of love and hope, and I was determined to send them one right back, no matter how simple.

Kids from the Tyngsboro elementary, middle, and high schools all sent cards and best wishes. My high school friends shared memories in their cards of hanging out with me, and whenever I read them, I got a little lost remembering the good times.

I knew there were more good memories to be made. I just needed to recover a little bit first.

Part of the recovery was learning, slowly and painfully, how to write by hand again. It was still weird to me that I couldn't hold a pen, but if I strapped it to my pointer finger, I could manage. It was not calligraphy. Actually, it looked like the work of a first grader.

This was the middle of February, so the first thing that this first grader wrote was a Valentine's Day letter to his mom.

She had been with me every step of the way from the first night in Boston. She could have slept in a separate hospital apartment that Shepherd provided her, but she spent every night in my room sleeping on a pull-out chair that didn't even go flat. Mom cared for me every morning and evening and was my support team when I wasn't working with staff. When I got back to my room after therapy, she was always there to ask questions, crack a joke, give me a hug, or offer me a snack. She fetched Frosty, walked down to the local gas station to buy candy, and begged the ICU nurses for another heated blanket. She helped me get into my manual chair late in the evening if I wanted to. She woke up in the middle of the night if I needed adjusting in bed. She would, and did, do anything for me.

At the same time, Mom definitely wanted me to figure things out on my own. She gave me just enough advice and asked just enough questions to get me thinking about solutions. One of her tricks was to drop random comments into a conversation during the day, and I'd find myself thinking about it at night. Maybe it seemed silly when she said it, but later on I realized how smart or thoughtful it was.

We spent a *lot* of time together. And sometimes the person who is there the most doesn't get enough credit. I mean, how can you possibly thank someone who does everything?

Mom had been through hell with me, and I needed to make her smile. These past weeks had been incredibly chaotic, and I wanted the Valentine's card to remind her that I was her son. Her grateful son.

The card just said "Happy Valentine's Day" in wobbly script, with "Love, Jack" beneath it, but it brought her to tears. Watching her cry was hard, but I knew I'd done the right thing as I watched her read and reread my little note. It was a very small thing, but for us, at this point in my recovery, it was huge.

Another night, more weirdness. But it's all me this time.

I'm on my back, rolling side to side in bed like a wave trying but failing to crash on a beach.

The funny thing is that if I succeeded, I'd be screwed. I'd flop onto my belly with hands and arms who knows where, too weak to sit up or roll back. It's probably just as well all I accomplish is slapping myself in the face.

On one of Dad's weekend visits, we went down to the Shepherd gym to see some of the USA Wheelchair Rugby Championship games. Dad had no idea the sport even existed. Who does, really? It's all part of the separate world that people in wheelchairs inhabit. But wheelchair rugby is cool. There's an amazing documentary about the USA team called *Murderball*. I highly recommend it, especially if you think that everyone in wheelchairs is weak and fragile. Dad was pretty shocked at the level of violence. Full contact is the norm, with wheelchairs tipping over and players crashing onto the hard basketball court floor. The chairs look pretty hard-core, all metallic and banged up like something out of *Mad Max*.

I wasn't ready for a death match in that arena, but I felt like I was already fighting for my life in the therapy gym. Transferring to a therapy mat from my chair was one of the biggest challenges. I had finally stopped relying on the Hoyer lift contraption and, with Cathi's help, had switched to a slide board. The slide board bridged my chair to the mat, and I (hypothetically) used my arms to slide my ass across it. Really, Cathi dragged me across, with the goal to eventually build up strength and do it myself.

I watched with jealousy as other teen patients with lower spinal injuries used their upper body to hoist themselves out of their chair. It tormented me to know that if my spine had shattered an inch or two lower, I'd have full use of my arms, hands, torso, all of it. Sometimes it seemed like there was a bigger difference between low and high spine injuries than there was between injured and uninjured people.

I spent endless hours on those therapy mats, most of them looking up at the ceiling. And I was grateful to find exactly what I had wished for in Lowell: a ceiling covered in artwork by former patients. In this, as in everything else, the Shepherd Center really understood the experience of being a patient.

Thankfully it wasn't ads from sponsors. It would be really cruel to force us to stare for hours at a logo for the Atlanta Falcons or a catheter company.

I got to know the artwork well. Some people painted their names or simple images, and others clearly spent some serious time doing intricate work. One patient drew Michael Jackson with incredible accuracy, while another one painted a fish jumping out of water. Many of the images had motivational quotes or phrases, and some were religious. I knew that before I left I, too, would leave my mark up there for future patients to see.

I have to admit that after a while I didn't want to see the messages anymore, because it meant that I was still stuck on my back like a baby. I spent a lot of time at the beginning of PT simply trying to roll over and push myself up. It was impossible at first.

Cathi placed one of my legs, with the knee bent, over the other leg, and I'd hold my folded arms close to my body and swing them over as hard as I could to get enough momentum to roll onto my side, hoping to get onto my stomach with my arms beneath me.

I failed hundreds of times. At first, I could roll over only an inch or two. At the end of my fifth week, my success rate was maybe 10 percent. The worst part, though, was hitting myself in the face over and over because I didn't have triceps to control the arm swing.

It sounds like a joke, but when you've punched yourself for the hundredth time, it's not that funny anymore.

To work on the push-up part, I first had to be able to prop myself up. Cathi supported me as I got up onto my elbows. At first I could only hold the position for a few seconds before my shoulders spasmed and gave out. But each day I stayed up a little longer.

I began to rebuild muscle in my shoulders with assisted push-ups. Cathi knelt over me and wrapped her arms around my chest as I pushed up a few inches on my elbows and then eased back down. I started with just a few, then gradually increased until finally Cathi was able to let go, and I could do a few on my own.

I was improving, but she explained that rolling over and sitting up were so fundamental to my future that I had to keep working on it throughout my time in Atlanta.

The few muscles I could still control had to be trained to make up the difference for all the others I'd lost. The years of gym time before the injury—cardio, strength training, bulking up—had disappeared along with my muscle mass. I weighed one hundred forty pounds, thirty pounds less than the day of the accident, but at least my weight had stabilized. I had stopped disappearing.

I had to work really hard just to make tiny improvements.

So I fought for progress even in bed after an exhausting day of therapy. The nights were long and being in bed was boring. If I wasn't watching TV or catching up on writing Thank You texts, I was exercising.

I worked especially hard on rolling over. Again and again I swung my arms over to reach my side. I probably looked like a crazy man rocking back and forth. But it was worth it if it built strength or gained a few inches. I never made it onto my stomach in bed, which was probably for the best, because if I had rolled over, I would have been stuck there until my mom flipped me like a one-hundred-forty-pound pancake.

I don't know for sure if it was motivation or optimism or anxiety or self-consciousness or all of the above that made me obsessively try to improve, but whatever it was it helped. It helped my state of mind to know I was doing all I could, and more importantly it helped me achieve some small victories.

I was able to put my toothbrush into the universal cuff, which meant I could brush my teeth by myself for the first time. It wasn't pretty, but I was flying solo and it felt good.

And I was able to load a fork or spoon in the cuff too. My arm movements had smoothed out, and eating had become easier, but I still didn't like the grip. The motion was centered on my palm instead of my fingers. So, Patty decided I was ready for the next step, a fork built with two loops at the end for my thumb and pointer finger. It didn't require the universal cuff, and the motion was much more natural. So now I could simply pick up a fork and eat.

This did wonders for my self-esteem, even if I was still a bit messy. I didn't need as much assistance to eat, and the way I used the fork looked more natural. People wouldn't see me struggle as much with every meal.

Then, like a reward for all the hard work, something amazing happened. I was lying in bed one evening, trying as usual to command a muscle, any muscle, to move. I didn't know if it was helping physically—it certainly hadn't succeeded so far—but it was my survival strategy.

And suddenly something sparked. It was a twitch in the right wrist joint where the muscles connected with ligament. When I tried to move the wrist, I saw my skin twitch a little bit. Then I waited. No twitch. Then I tried to move again and there was the twitch. And then—*Yes!*—I had a twitch in my left wrist as well.

And so it begins, I thought.

I wouldn't have full wrist movement anytime soon. Recovering neurological function isn't like flipping a switch. It starts with the smallest of movements and takes months to become really noticeable. So as soon as I saw that twitching, I knew I had to bust my ass to build on the success. I didn't really want to make a big deal out of this until I had made some real progress.

Still, though, that first twitch sent me over the edge. It felt like I'd been marooned on an island for a month and then saw a ship. I knew I wasn't saved yet, but things were looking up. I had a huge smile on my face and looked around to see if Mom had seen it happen. She hadn't, but she was so excited when I told her. Like me, even though she had been waiting for stuff like this to happen, she was amazed when it finally did.

All my optimism that I would earn some breakthroughs had finally paid off. And I really needed the boost. The daily grind of OT and PT without big successes had been hard.

Now I knew that I wouldn't need wrist braces for the rest of my life. I would eventually be able to do a lot more with my hands. It was the smallest of accomplishments, yet it felt so huge. I wasn't making Neil Armstrong's famous footprint on the Moon or taking a leap for mankind, but I felt like I was a step closer to going home. I couldn't wait to see what would move next.

6
GOOD NEWS

Good things really do happen in the midst of bad times. Friends visit, you make a good joke, a muscle twitches, a crowd cheers. But it's hard sometimes to know what the good stuff means. Is Sisyphus making progress or fooling himself? Is Alice making friends or going insane?

Maybe I should stop thinking about it and simply enjoy it while it lasts.

I became obsessed with expanding my wrist movement, both in OT with Patty and on my own. Every day Patty hooked me up to the Bioness hand stimulator, which sent electrical impulses through my forearms into my hands and fingers. Every night I tried to put some more life into the twitch.

As my wrists strengthened and gained range of motion, I was able to start picking things up with tenodesis. Tenodesis is a replacement for the normal action of grabbing something with your fingers. Instead, you bend your wrist backward to make your fingers curl up in a grasping motion. Once I practiced enough, I could use it to grab my cell phone, water bottle, whatever.

As I expanded my ability to use my hands, I got rid of the mobile arm support. That, in turn, was progress toward taking on two of my biggest personal challenges: bathing and dressing myself. Both were impossible to do alone, but I wanted to do as much as I could.

The day came when Patty and I were scheduled to work on showering. This is one of the simple things you take for granted when you have a healthy spine, but it becomes really hard after an SCI. I won't talk too much about washing myself because, really, how often do people talk to you about how they soap up and rinse off? I didn't really want to get into it with Patty, but I had to. And she was so respectful of me and my needs that I knew it would be okay.

What I didn't expect was Patty showing up in my room with floaties on her arms and a ducky ring around her waist. In fact, that was the first thing I saw when I opened my eyes at seven a.m. It's not easy to get a teenager with an SCI to crack up that early in the morning, but Patty had a gift for making things less depressing.

As for dressing myself, putting on pants was way beyond me, so I started with my shirt. I was too weak to lift my arms over my head, find the armholes, and pull the shirt down the way I used to. So my early shirt strategy was similar to my early power chair technique: go full speed ahead and see what happens. I put the shirt in my lap and wiggled my hands through it, then flung my arms above my head and hoped that the whole thing fell down over my head. More often than not I missed by a mile and ended up as a man conquered by his shirt. On rare occasions, though, I got it and it felt like a hole-in-one in golf.

I spent my evenings trying to get it off. Without triceps, I couldn't sneak my arms back through the holes and out through the bottom of the shirt. I tried hard, though, rocking back and forth for ten minutes until I ended up exhausted and out of breath. Finally I solved it by putting one arm under the shirt and pushing on the other arm hole while I pulled the second arm through. It took about fifteen minutes at first. I would get better, I knew, but I really needed my triceps to come back.

And right on cue, I had my next breakthrough.

I was in for my weekly visit with Cheryl in her tiny office. Her background was in OT, so she ran me through two tests to look for recovered triceps function. First, she held my wrist and put the fingers of her other hand on one of the three heads of the triceps, then told me to contract the muscle as hard as I could while she felt for a reaction. Then she moved to the next head, and then the next. I noticed Cheryl was smiling. Then to the other arm. She was still smiling.

"It's there," Cheryl said. "You've got triceps."

Better yet, I was symmetrical. The response was weak, but it was similar in both arms. A lot of SCI patients aren't so lucky.

The second test was quicker. Cheryl held my arm horizontal, palm down, while she supported the elbow. Then she asked me to try to lift my forearm up, which in an able-bodied arm activates the triceps against gravity.

We knew I couldn't lift the forearm, but she had her fingertips on the triceps to feel for any action. And again—amazing!—she felt a twitch as the muscle made a small contraction.

This was huge, or huger than huge. If—no, not if—*when* I developed my triceps back to fuller function, I'd be able to reach so many of my goals. And to literally reach for things. I took it personally every time someone had to hold a water bottle for me.

I wanted to beat this injury and get my life back. Not my old life, necessarily. I was slowly realizing that might not be possible, but I wanted my independence. I wanted, at the very least, to be putting on my pants and to be cruising around in a manual chair. Anything short of that I considered unsatisfactory.

It's a measure of how serious I was about getting better that I wasn't super ecstatic about these little triceps movements. I wanted more, expected more, and was competing—against my-self? Against fate?—for more. Don't get me wrong. I was happy, but not as happy as I knew my parents would be.

I told Mom as soon as I got back to the room. She was thrilled and gave me a hug. Now I had to call Dad. Every time I talked with him on the phone or saw how he looked at me, I could tell how upset he still was. His kid was hurt and had an uncertain future. The emotion was still raw. I was so happy to be able to give him some good news.

I dialed his number.

"Hey, Jack. What's up? How are you doing?"

"Dad, I can move my triceps."

Silence. Not a word.

I could hear the relief and joy in his breathing on the other end of the phone. I don't want to accuse the infamous Bill Trottier of choking up, but I could feel some weight floating off his shoul-ders in that moment. I know he felt like his prayers were being answered. He and Mom knew that functional triceps would give me a better life than they feared I'd have.

He broke the silence, finally, with a vague noise before clearing his throat.

"This is amazing, Jack. I'm really excited for you," he said.

Through muddled emotions he said he was proud of me and that this was big news.

The joy this brought my parents inspired me during the rest of my recovery in Atlanta. After that moment in Cheryl's office, there wasn't a day I didn't work my triceps as hard as I could. I never took time off. The recovered function was a constant reminder that at least some aspects of this injury were temporary.

More good news: the Shepherd staff decided I was finally ready to get rid of the big plastic cervical neck brace. That was another hallelujah moment, since I hated that thing like a dog hates a cone of shame.

Every little victory was an affirmation of my efforts and a step in the right direction. I was moving along the path toward independence by tackling one small problem at a time.

It was nearly March 1, five weeks into my time in Atlanta, and the day of Justin and Derek's arrival. I don't think I was so ready for anything in my whole life. All the patience I had developed to deal with my slow-ass recovery went out the window. That whole day of waking up and being dressed and doing two sessions of therapy and eating meals with a special fork and all of this serious, abnormal stuff that had taken over my life . . . I wanted it to disappear so the clock could hit six p.m. and bring those guys to my room. They were my first non-family visitors since I settled into the Shepherd Center, but more importantly they were my best friends. It meant the world to me that they had traveled two thousand miles to hang out.

The moment I saw them come through the doorway was the first time in weeks that I felt normal. I was instantly transported back home to the good old days. I had so many memories wrapped up in these guys that when they showed up, I was that kid again.

Not someone with an injury or disability but a friend.

Sometimes I think friendship is proof that we have a soul. The connection and the love feel like they will outlast our bodies.

That Friday evening felt like I was back in my basement shooting the shit, laughing, and joking with my friends. I had missed our time together so much. Now, for a whole weekend, I didn't have to have serious conversations about my body that pissed me off or made me sad.

I gave them a tour of the hospital, and then we spent the entire night hanging out in my room. Normally after a certain amount of time a conversation dries up and we do something else or go home. But there was something perfect about that night. We had so much to say to each other—it was hilarious and stupid and beautiful—and I don't think I've talked so much in my whole life. We ended up stealing another fold-out chair from a room down the hall so they could both crash in my room. My mom slept in the apartment.

I managed to get up at my normal time for Saturday OT, but I slept through the whole session—the bonus to having no physical sensation!—as the weekend therapist hooked up my arms to the Bioness unit. She woke me at the end, unplugged me, and sent me back to my room where I took a three-hour nap. It was the only day during my whole stay at Shepherd when I felt like a slacker.

Derek and Justin delivered messages of support from a bunch of friends back home. I was still receiving cards and texts and gifts by the boatload but hearing it from those two in my room was a really powerful reminder that people were still thinking about me.

Coincidentally, a major fundraiser had been scheduled for this weekend at the Tyngsboro Sports Center. We decided that the guys would be at my side when I FaceTimed in to talk to the crowd. The space had been donated by the owners, the Wickens family, whose kids I knew from school. This was our second fundraiser since the accident. The Greg Hill morning show on WAAF in Boston raised almost $30,000 for me before I left for Atlanta.

It's not easy to be on the receiving end of so much kindness, but my family knew there was no way around it. The treatment costs in Boston and Atlanta—about a million dollars—were covered by insurance, as was the medical equipment I'd need at home, but renovating the house was on us. And we had no idea what other expenses would come our way.

Not to mention that my parents had suddenly upended their working lives to help me. Dad worked seven to five every day at Wayside Ford and then renovated the house until ten p.m. most nights, and Mom hadn't been back to work at Watermark Environmental in Lowell since the day of the accident. But her company had been amazing, with her boss holding her job open and her colleagues donating their vacation time so Mom's paychecks kept coming in even though she was at my side in Atlanta.

A friend in town, Barry Dick, is a financial advisor who was helping to coordinate donations to the Get Jack Better Fund. He told Mom, "I don't want you worrying about finances while you're with Jack. Just send your bills to me, and I'll use the donations to take care of them." Mom had forwarded all of our Tyngsboro mail to Shepherd Center, so whenever a phone bill or insurance payment came in, she simply sent it to Barry. He was true to his word. All our bills were paid for.

It's impossible to overstate this: The whole community stunned us with their generosity. In many ways, my recovery would not have been possible without the love and support of the people of Tyngsboro.

Even so, this March 2 event at the sports center blew me away. The building can hold 1,200 people but they sold 1,500 tickets. The gathering started well before we got connected, with hundreds of people milling around on the plastic grass of the indoor field, putting raffle tickets into buckets next to donated prizes. I saw a video later of the whole thing and was really moved when a woman who lived near us said she didn't know me but "it's a story that hit everyone hard. We're out here showing our support."

A lot of folks were wearing our black fundraising T-shirts that said "STAY STRONG" and "TYNGSBORO TOUGH" on the front. On the back there was a big red 7 (my football number) and *Jack* written over it in cursive. This became my brand after the accident. My family used it on everything, including thank-you cards for donations and gifts.

When the lights dimmed in preparation for the video link, Dad took the microphone and started by reading some thank yous from Mom. Sam stood next to him lighting the text with her phone. They were both wearing the black *Jack/7* T-shirts. Mom wanted to thank Nashoba Valley, which had done some fundraising with "I Ride for Jack" stickers and sweatshirts, and she wanted to acknowledge the vast network of people on social media that had brought in so many offers of support.

But mainly she wanted to say this: "I'd like to thank my daughter Samantha. She and Jack are as close as two siblings can be, and I don't think she realizes how much she influences him and keeps him strong. She constantly offers her help and has done so much for him back home. We both miss her terribly and look forward to her visits. We love you, Sam." The audience cheered and clapped while Sam looked embarrassed and emotional at the same time.

It's true about how much I missed Sam, though. It really

seemed like the sun came out in Atlanta every time she visited.

Then Dad started speaking for himself: "When something . . ." He paused. "When something bad happens to your kid . . . You know, everyone thinks, *I'm glad it's not me*, and wonders, *What would I do?*" He looked around. "Well, this is what you do. You jump to it. You put everything aside, and you get the job done. You do what's best for your kids. You think you do it on a daily basis, but when it comes over the top like this, you step it up and you put it into high gear. And Chris did just that. She put her life on hold, she put her job on hold, to travel down to Atlanta with Jack. She spent every night with him in Boston Children's Hospital, and she's spending every night with him at the Shepherd Center." That got a huge round of applause.

Which was Mom's cue. The video link was live, and she was ready. She had put on a black turtleneck and written out her little speech on cards and taped them below the laptop. She was sitting on my knees to block the audience's view of me, but they could see Derek and Justin on either side.

Mom mainly wanted to make sure everyone knew how much Dad was doing too. "Even though he's so far away, Bill has been a huge part of Jack's recovery. He comes down when he can. He takes part in every conference, he speaks directly to Jack's therapist and case workers, and he talks to me and Jack every day." At this point I could hear her voice starting to crack, which wasn't a surprise. Crying had become normal for her through the nightmare of the last several weeks. She was tough, but she was honest with her feelings too.

Now, though, I knew she really didn't want to break down in front of the crowd, so I was quietly poking her from behind, whispering, "Unicorns and beaches, Mom. Unicorns and puppies.

Don't cry now."

Which seemed to help. She took a breath and went on, "Bill has coached Jack to be the best athlete he can be, and now he's taken the same approach to Jack's recovery." The audience cheered again.

Now she smiled, stood up, and before stepping off camera with a big mock flourish, said, "And now, without further ado . . . my three sons!" Other than the reference to the ancient TV show, the joke was that Justin and Derek really were like adopted kids, since they were at our house all the time. They were like brothers who got all the same love and discipline but had to sleep somewhere else.

It was my turn. I had done some thinking about this. I gave the cheering crowd a big smile and a floppy wave, and then as they quieted I said, in a big stage voice, "Hey guys, how's it hanging?" Which is a pretty goofy thing to ask hundreds of people, but I'd decided that the first thing I said to the good people of Tyngsboro should show them that I hadn't changed, that I was still the same easy-going Jack but in a different circumstance. I wanted to put them at ease. They seemed to like it.

I wanted to make myself feel a little better too. If everyone had a good impression of me, then maybe I'd have less to worry about when I went home.

We'd decided that the boys would say a quick hello before I took over. So Justin, who's pretty comfortable in front of the camera, spoke up, "Hi everyone. I just wanted to say that since day one, with this guy right here, on the lacrosse field . . . You know, I had his back on the field and I have his back right now." He put his hand on my shoulder. "He's been doing great since the last time I saw him in Boston." The crowd cheered.

Then it was Derek's turn. He was a bit nervous and made it

quick. "It's good to be here to see our best friend, and he's doing good, so I'll let you guys talk now."

I could hear someone in the audience say, "A man of few words . . ."

My turn again. I gave everyone my biggest Happy Patient smile and said, "Heeeeeyyyy . . . ," as the cheers for Derek were fading. The crowd laughed and then quieted, since finally it was time to get a little more serious.

Justin and Derek and I only saw Dad and Sam and Ian, but it was crazy to occasionally get a glimpse of the crowd and to hear the roar when they cheered.

Dad asked, "Hey, Jack, can you hear me?"

"I can," I said.

"Why don't you tell everybody—why don't you give them an idea of what a day is like for you down there, how hard you're working in OT and PT. Give them a little glimpse."

"All right. Well, um . . ." I'll save you the details, but I gave them a summary of my schedule and the workouts.

Then, as always, I lightened things up a bit. "That's pretty much a typical day here. Mess around, throw a few parties." The crowd laughed, and the three of us cracked up.

Dad kept it going. "Hey, I want you to tell everybody how you're feeling, give them an idea . . . Where's your neck brace, by the way? Did you lose it?"

"Yeah, I lost it this week," I said, and then felt a little embarrassed and proud as I heard everybody clap and cheer.

Dad was getting into his role of master of ceremonies. He wanted to hit the audience with all the highlights. "Hey, what's up? What's goin' on? You got some news about some part of your arms that's starting to move again. What's goin' on with those?

Tell us about it."

"Well, as you can see"—I moved my hand up and down—"I got my wrists back." The crowd roared. All I could do was smile and shake my head.

Dad said, "Hey, this is big stuff in Tyngsboro, kid, let me tell ya!" My smile got bigger as I thought about what that meant. Small town, strong community.

And I had more news. "I started to get my triceps back. That started last week."

I could hear something Sam was whispering near the microphone, even though the Tyngsboro Sports Center was getting pretty raucous, "Triceps! Huge, huge, huge." That felt pretty good too.

"Hey, Jack, why don't you tell them what we've been talking about? What are our three favorite words right now for you?"

"Don't be lazy."

"Don't be lazy, that's right!" Dad replied. "You're working hard day and night, right?"

It was great to hear my dad being proud of me in front of the crowd, making them cheer again and again. He was coaching me, too, using the fundraiser to keep me motivated and making sure I felt connected to the town that had embraced me. Together, we were giving them a show, but the show was for me too.

Finally, the show ended. There was a huge "One, two, three!" and a final big cheer from the masses in the packed fitness center. It was a hell of a sign-off.

When the connection finally cut, Justin, Derek, and I gave each other a that-was-cool look. I didn't feel like I had a lot to show for my time in Atlanta, especially compared to what I had hoped would happen, but Dad told me later that people in the sports center were impressed by how far I had come in such a short time. I heard also that some people had feared the worst, like seeing me bedridden and plugged into machines. Mostly, though, I think they were surprised by the smile on my face.

It's hard to say how much of that smile was my positive attitude and how much was the fact that I'd spent twenty-four hours laughing with my two best friends. I know how to put on a good show, but it was probably more of the latter.

As for the rest of the weekend, remember Tom Hanks's character in *Saving Private Ryan* telling Matt Damon's character that he had this special memory of his wife in the garden and that memory is what kept him sane during the chaos of war? Remember also that he said he wasn't going to share it, because it was too precious? That's how I feel about my time with Derek and Justin.

We were so in the moment and there was so much we talked about, but really all that mattered was that we were saying it. Being together was bigger than the words we said. I felt alive and connected. And connected to home.

I like being one of only three people who shared that experience. I got to take a break from reality and have a little bit of fun for once. I didn't think of myself as a quadriplegic but more like the same old Jack of two months ago.

It's like baseball's All-Star break, when the players take a week off to have fun and rest up before having to get back to the second half of the season. I was able to set everything aside and be the kid I was "supposed" to be. Having my friends there lifted me up and freed me from my limitations in a way I could never express. It's hard to say much more about it, so I won't.

7

LIKE PICKING UP A NEW SPORT

I hope someone finds me soon. Paper feels nice and smooth on my face, but it's pretty thin for a pillow.

It's kind of cool to see everything on my desk up close—only a few inches away from my nose—because I feel like some tiny explorer lost between the books and fast-food bags. But it's getting a bit old.

I've been here for a while, and I don't know when anyone will notice that I'm stuck.

Back home, my *Jack/7* shirts were showing up everywhere. People wore them around town, and the Tyngsboro girls' basketball team wore them during warm-ups before their games. Then one night at a boys' basketball game, the Dracut players walked in wearing them too. Dracut is a neighboring town, but still I was amazed that another team showed that much consideration. It's one of the things I love about sports. Good coaches teach players about respect and the importance of ritual.

Meanwhile, back in Atlanta, I had a new friend named Rommel, a massive Rottweiler who helped kids like me learn new tricks. After I exhausted myself switching from the chair to the mat on the slide board, Rommel gave me my reward: hopping up next to me to be petted. There really is something about a dog's unconditional love that makes life better.

And Rommel motivated me. At first, I could only pet him a few times. My arm burnt out that quickly. Each session with him was a little better, though, and soon I was worthy of sharing his toys. Well, barely. His trainer had a ball for me to throw. It had a couple holes I could put my fingers in to help me grab it, but the release was tricky. At first the ball plopped down at my feet. Rommel was very polite about this and then very cheerful when the ball finally went some distance across the gym.

I never thought hanging out with a dog would be hard work—except maybe when I was ninety years old or something—but I didn't care. I could have played with that huge, sweet dog all day. It took my mind off the injury and reminded me of my own sweet dog, Bode, a little light-brown boxer with a dark face. We got Bode during the 2006 winter Olympics and named him after our favorite skier, Bode Miller, who was from New Hampshire. I couldn't wait to see my dog again.

Back in my room watching TV after working with Rommel for the first time, I felt the right side of my face grow strangely warm. Then I noticed that the right side of my chest and back all the way down to my right hand were becoming wet with sweat as well. My left side was cool and dry.

I shouldn't have been sweating at all. With my complete C6 break, I couldn't thermoregulate (which is why I was constantly feeling cold) and I couldn't sweat. My spine wasn't passing messages about temperature in either direction.

Swelling from a spinal injury can take up to two years to subside. When it subsides, there is the possibility of some healing and return of sensation. It's normal for the return of feeling to begin on one side or the other, but it's almost impossible that a function like sweating would return in two months instead of two years.

Dr. Murray suspected it was instead a symptom of autonomic dysreflexia (AD), which is a complicated name for how a spine-injured body responds to a problem in an area that no longer communicates with the brain. Think of it as setting off a fire alarm in a whole building to let people know you're trapped in the basement.

The problem, which could be as minor as a tight shoe, sets off a reaction that creates a spike in blood pressure. Because the information highway through my spine was shut down, there was no way for the brain to signal the body to reduce the blood pressure. So all we could do was try to find and fix the problem. Sometimes we succeeded by emptying my bladder or bowels, but that could drop my blood pressure like a stone and almost make me pass out.

Since I mentioned bladder and bowels, I suppose it's time I get a bit personal. I don't want to cross the line into TMI, but there's no shame in this stuff either. You're probably curious how being paralyzed affects daily functions. Any spinal injury impacts bladder control, and spinal injuries above L1 (that's the top vertebra in your lower back) causes upper motor neuron syndrome, which basically means my intestines work fine but I don't have voluntary control over bowel movements. Since my first day at the Shepherd Center, I've used catheters to pee and been on a bowel program. I'll save you the graphic details, but just know it's weird and annoying to play doctor with your own body every day.

A return to normal bowel and bladder function is at the top of the wish list for anyone with a complete spinal injury. It's one thing to require a chair to get around, but to have to spend so much time and effort to go to the bathroom is a pain in the . . . well, you get it.

As for the sweating, we never did fix it. My team eventually figured that the red alert was just the spine trying to heal itself. In some patients, constant or severe AD leads to serious heart damage, hospitalization, or even death. Luckily, I wasn't dealing with that or the chronic headaches that are typical for AD sufferers, but we had to figure out a solution to the sweating because it was making me even colder. So cold, in fact, that I was having a hard time even participating in therapy. I lay there on the mat shivering while trying to do my exercises, while all I could think about was how cold I was.

After most sessions and before going to bed, I needed a bunch of heated blankets wrapped around me, even though the temperature in my room was set above seventy degrees. At first I had to ask for the blankets, but the nurses soon had them ready as soon as I got back. Rebecca, Frosty's owner, always slipped into the ICU to get the warmest ones she could find. Sometimes even that wasn't enough, though, and I struggled to fall asleep because I was shivering so much.

One thing that kept me a little warmer was a quilt that had been made by the grandmother of one of my classmates and signed by about a hundred people. It was covered in little messages wishing me luck and sending me love. Dad brought it down with him on the plane. There were two messages on it that really meant a lot to me.

Sam wrote "Like picking up a new sport," which cut through a lot of my anxiety. Sure, this was a life-changing event, but it was also a new challenge, and Sam knew how a sports challenge kept me focused. She has always known what to say to me.

The other note was from my buddy Adam. He drew a little picture of two stick figures sitting at a desk together and wrote, "I *miss* this, bro." Seeing it broke me down. Adam and I shared a lab table together in Anatomy and Physiology, and we had so much fun joking around (maybe a little too much fun, if I'm being honest), and I knew what he meant about missing it. What had been a highlight of my school day was now just one more item on the long list of things I had left behind.

Like normal sweating.

It was just my luck that the sweating was on my dominant right side. Here I was, struggling to handle everything with a clumsy, and now sweaty, right hand. I couldn't even shake someone's hand without worrying about it. "Hey, sorry about the slimy flipper!"

It took a while to find a way to treat the sweating. A cold face cloth was a logical solution, but not only did it fail to help but it made it worse. Plus I felt like an icicle. Finally out of desperation we tried heat, and that did wonders. It was a win-win, with an immediate stop to the sweating and a boost for my core temperature as a bonus. But as soon as the warm towel or blanket cooled down, the sweating and shivering came back.

And it didn't help that the sweating was brought on by some of my therapies, especially the FES bike. Functional electrical stimulation is pretty much what it sounds like, a machine that sends signals through small electrodes to your leg muscles to fire in a sequence that mimics pedaling a bike. It stimulated my hip flexors and quads to bring my leg up and then my calf muscle and hamstring to bring it back down, alternating left and right legs.

It was a pretty awesome confidence booster to spend an hour at a time pedaling away with my headphones on and a view out the window to the real world. I felt normal and able-bodied, if only for an hour. Maybe I didn't look so normal with a hot towel wrapped around my head, but I didn't care.

Sometimes my confidence got a little ahead of itself, though. Hanging out in my room before the afternoon therapy session, I really wanted a piece of gum. My mom was away on an errand, and the gum was at the very back of the desk. I brought the power chair up alongside the desk and stretched for the gum, but no luck. *No problem*, I thought, *I have triceps*.

Figuring I'd grab the gum and push myself back toward the chair, I lunged as hard as I could. Big mistake. My upper body was now sprawled out on the desk, and my face was plopped down on some paperwork. I had no core muscles or legs to pull me back into the chair and, sadly, not nearly enough triceps power to force a retreat. My arms were in front of me, my hands inches short of the gum. Definitely a lose-lose situation. All I could do was lie there staring at the debris on the desk.

It reminded me of some recent crazy dreams. I was trying so hard to run, but I couldn't. The surface was deep sand or soft pillows or something impossible to run on. I woke up each time with mixed feelings. Maybe I wasn't going anywhere, but at least I was running.

And now all I could really do was laugh. I wasn't angry or disappointed. I was actually proud of myself for making the attempt. I had to lie there like a cat on the desk and wait for someone to rescue me, and thankfully after about ten minutes a nurse walked by my open door and did a double take before coming in to pull me back into the chair.

Lots of odd things happen in the adolescent section at Shepherd, I'm sure, so she wasn't too fazed. But we were both so focused on settling me back into my chair that she left the room before I remembered to ask her to get me the piece of gum.

In other entertainment news, one of the night-shift nurses, Artica Jackson, had a good sense of humor and liked to mess with us, sometimes moving our things around while we slept. She even tossed toilet paper all over my room one night near the end of my time on the inpatient floor. I could not let this go unpunished. I conspired with Taylor—the other Boston Boy—and decided that we were going to get our revenge on Artica by messing with her car. Sarah, our recreational therapist, agreed to be in on the prank. She got back late one night from an outing with other patients to an Atlanta Braves game and then woke me up at eleven p.m. before we both went to get Taylor. The three of us snuck out into the parking garage with two rolls of industrial-sized Saran Wrap. It was a total comedy scene, with two guys in wheelchairs (me in an automatic and Taylor in a manual) shrink-wrapping a really nice-looking BMW while our therapist acted as lookout. We hooked the plastic on and wrapped the car several times until the doors and windows were entirely covered.

Then, right as we took our last lap of the car, the alarm went off. The noise was deafening inside the concrete walls of the garage. We panicked and booked it back to the elevator, Taylor and I dying with laughter as we headed back to our rooms. It was a terrific revenge.

Artica gave me a nice bless-your-heart smile the following evening, and mentioned she was lucky to have had medical scissors in her purse. Supposedly it didn't take too long to get the wrap off her car, but I still wish I could have been there to see her face.

I imagine her walking to her car at the end of her long shift, just wanting to go home but stopping and staring when she found her BMW wrapped up like a piece of fruit. That's one of my favorite memories of Atlanta.

Another nice memory is the Red Sox pummeling the Yankees in the season opener on April 1. Of course I watched it with Cathi. The PT room has a TV with a Wii gaming system used as a fun therapy by patients with recovering upper body function. For me, the TV was emotional therapy, since the game wasn't even close. The Sox scored eight runs on thirteen hits, while the Yankees struggled to get two runs on six hits. A bonus was that the Yankees lost at Yankee Stadium. After every Sox hit, I gave Cathi a look like, "You saw that, right?" She did her best to give me shit every time the Yankees got on base, but there wasn't too much of that. It was a fun back and forth. Little did we know it was the start of a season that had the Red Sox winning the World Series and the Yankees having their worst season since long before I was born.

I took it as a sign of good things to come.

And sure enough, I finally put my shirt on without a struggle a few days later. Patty started clapping. I smiled. Major milestone accomplished.

Speaking of milestones, it was finally time to paint my ceiling tile. I'm no artist, but what I wanted to do wasn't complicated. I had to paint my *Jack/7* logo. I wanted my art to represent not only me but also the people back home who had used that logo to support my family. Patty stuck a paintbrush into the universal cuff on my right hand, and I used my left to keep it steady. The tile was in my lap. I was careful, because I was afraid they wouldn't give me another tile to work on. I think it came out pretty well, and I hope it's still up there.

On April 13, the end of my inpatient stay, my team held a twenty-minute graduation ceremony for me in the therapy room. I had seen others go through it, and now it was my turn. It was a bittersweet moment, for sure. The weeks had flown by, but at the same time I felt like I had been there forever. I was super nervous about going home. I didn't know if I'd be able to continue recovery on my own, yet here I was leaving the best hospital in the country for SCIs.

I still had two weeks in the outpatient clinic before I had to officially say goodbye, but really I would hardly see any of these people again. I was moving out of the hospital and would have a new team of therapists. The good news was that in a month Patty was coming to Tyngsboro to help with my reintroduction to school, so with her at least it was less of a goodbye and more of a "See you later . . ."

Patty, Cathi, Sarah, Cheryl, and Rebecca were all there, plus a handful of patients. Frosty tried to jump into my lap for the group photo. The staff honored me with a blue T-shirt that said "SHEPHERD BOOT CAMP," and in turn I signed the basketball and wooden block I'd been given by earlier graduates before handing them off to others. I tried to throw a bounce pass with the basketball to Taylor, but the ball just hit the footplate of my chair and rolled off to the side. I gave him a look and said, "I tried," which was good for a laugh anyway.

The gift exchange might seem kind of silly, but it was a nice symbolic way to support each other and to feel rewarded for our hard work. We're the only ones who know how difficult it is to adjust to this new life, so when we do little things for each other it means a lot.

Some of my team stood up to talk about me. It was the kind

of respectful, supportive stuff you expect. You know, how hard I worked, my accomplishments compared to where I started. But they weren't afraid to poke fun at me too. The best moment was when Patty crawled onto one of the PT mats with a bunch of blankets and started shivering like she was dying of hypothermia. It was pretty funny seeing it through her eyes. That I could cheerfully watch my OT make fun of me and my SCI symptoms in front of an audience says a lot about the special relationship I had with Patty.

But I want to say also how ridiculously smart Patty was too. She was probably the smartest person I've ever met and could rattle off anatomy and physiology terms like crazy. Patty was so bubbly and funny that I forgot there was a science to what she did. She manufactured my wrist braces and found the mobile arm support that transformed my ability to communicate. She could explain the science and the therapeutic theory to me in a way that made it easy to understand.

Cathi came over to talk privately, which was more her style. She became really serious and very sincere about the progress I had made. I had started with nothing, she said, but through real determination I had given myself a promising future.

Cathi was a natural coach, which made her perfect for a guy like me. While some great athletes never have great coaches, many do. I think the same holds true for therapists and their clients. I worked hard, but Cathi made me give that extra 10 percent. She could tell if I was slacking or if I was tired, but she didn't care. She wanted progress, and she got it.

Cathi told me how proud she was of how much I'd accomplished. Then she reiterated it, to emphasize that she truly meant it, and that she wasn't merely saying something she had said to many patients before me. We locked eyes, and I really believed what she was saying. She made it seem like our time together had done as much for her as it did for me. Cathi was amazingly genuine like that. It was just like her to make this little ceremony something personal and meaningful. I'll never forget that moment.

I looked at Cathi and Patty and the others and said, "Thank you for everything. I wouldn't be where I am without you, and I'll never forget you." It wasn't enough, but how could I ever express enough gratitude for their efforts in giving me some of my life back? I was pretty sure that over time I'd realize how much of an impact they had on my life and my recovery, and that my gratitude would continue to grow.

I owed my life to these people, so it was hard to say goodbye. It was hard also because I was nervous, but they assured me that I was ready.

Finally, it was time for me to contribute to the collection of inspirational quotes from every person who has graduated inpatient. There's a whiteboard in the gym that slowly becomes covered with these quotes as patients move on. Once the board is filled up, one of the staff types all of it onto a piece of paper, posts it on the wall, and erases the board, and then the process starts over. There were a few years of quotes typed out and probably a year's worth on the board.

So what could I say that summarized my successes, my strategies for recovery, and my physical and emotional survival tactics? I didn't have to think too hard. My advice to everyone wheeling into that gym in the days and years after I left was simple: don't be lazy.

8

DREAMS AND NIGHTMARES

I just want to be alone for a while to figure this out and get better. I want to hide in a cave for a year where I can make my slow-ass progress without everyone watching.

When I get frustrated, the angels who are helping me become annoying witnesses to my failure.

Before I got to Atlanta, I had pictured my rehabilitation process to be an action movie. The longer I've been here the more it feels like late night C-SPAN 3.

I had spent eleven weeks in the Shepherd Center's inpatient ward and was desperate to see Tyngsboro again, but my family and I had agreed with the staff, especially Patty, who thought I should do two final weeks of therapy in their outpatient facility. It would be a transition period and a test for all of us. We'd practice living without 24/7 hospital care but still would have the staff on hand if we needed help. My parents would practice caring for my daily needs without a nurse looking over their shoulder.

Mom and I moved out of the regular hospital into an attached apartment building.

I liked the location change since it felt both a little like independence and like one small step toward Tyngsboro. It did feel little weird living someplace that wasn't home or a hospital, and it smelled like disinfectant, but I wouldn't be there long. The apartment was simple, with a combo living room/kitchen/dining room, a bathroom with a walk-in (or wheel-in) shower, and a bedroom with a single bed and my hospital bed.

Each morning Mom (or Dad if he was visiting) helped me get up, dress, and prepare for the day, but I insisted on making the trip to the outpatient gym on my own. I had to train myself for independent living, even if "independent" in this case was only a five-minute commute down a long hallway and through the parking garage back into the main building.

I have to confess that at first I got off the hospital elevator at the wrong floor. My old inpatient gym was on the fourth floor, and the outpatient gym was on the second floor. For some reason I kept going to the third floor, which is the brain injury unit. No jokes, please. It was pretty obviously the wrong floor, since the lights were turned down low to prevent headaches. The hallway outside the elevator looked kind of horror-movie creepy, and since I was wandering on my own, I learned not to make that mistake again.

I was now in a bigger gym with more people around, many of them adults dealing with their SCI. I talked with a few guys who were a year or so past their injury, including a twenty-five-year-old who was still figuring out the details of living in an apartment with his girlfriend. He was living independently, but it was complicated. If he was my future, then the future looked . . . difficult. My injury, if it didn't improve, might make it harder to meet someone, start a relationship, fall in love, and build a family. But I couldn't worry about that yet.

I had a new set of therapists. Which was weird. They were as knowledgeable as the inpatient crew, but I missed Cathi and Patty. Even though I'd spent three months in the same building, I felt like I was starting all over again.

Our focus still was training me to dress myself and switch over to a manual chair. I had made good progress in strengthening my biceps and shoulders and in recovering strength in my wrists and triceps, but it was slow and there was a lot to do. I needed more muscle and some new strategies, especially if I wanted to meet my greatest challenge: get my damn pants on.

We decided I should try to get dressed in bed rather than the chair. But I first needed to be able to sit up on my own. And this became the main task of my outpatient therapy. I tried grabbing the rails to pull myself up, but no matter how hard I tried, I didn't have the strength.

Then we tied one end of a tether to the foot of the bed. I put my arm through a loop at the other end and put the burden on my bicep muscle. All in one motion I rolled to one side and pulled as hard as I could to try to get myself up.

For the first few days of outpatient therapy that's all I worked on. I never touched a piece of clothing. I did hundreds of reps to get into the seated position. I failed over and over. Without my abs, I was still a limp noodle stretched out on the bed.

This was pissing me off. I decided to innovate. And by "innovate" I mean cheat a little. It took me a week to remember I was still in a hospital bed, which has its perks, specifically the buttons along the inside of the railings to control the height of the head and feet.

All I had to do was push a button and lift the head of the bed a little. Then it was much easier to get fully upright. So that's what I did. But first I had to be able to push the button. I inched my way over to the edge of the bed using my head and elbows while still lying on my back. After a few attempts I finally got close enough to push the buttons with one of my knuckles.

With the head of the bed elevated it was ten times easier to hook my arm through the tether and pull myself up. But I couldn't stay up. I had learned with Cathi how to throw my arms back and prop myself, and I'd gotten stronger but not strong enough to prop with one arm and get my pants on with the other.

Progress in the manual chair, too, was being measured in inches rather than miles. I still spent most of my time in the power chair—I needed the option to tilt back when I had low blood pressure—so I knew that I wouldn't be in the manual when I got home.

I prepared for using the power chair at home by practicing in the wheelchair obstacle course in the outpatient courtyard. It wasn't some kind of Spartan Race but just some difficult sections of sidewalk made up of a step, a gravel patch, a sand trap, and some grass. The first time I saw it I pleaded with my mom to be my spotter but didn't wait for an answer. I drove into the gravel at full speed and got stuck.

Mom wasn't ready. "Jack, stop! Let's wait for someone to show you how! Back up! Go forward! What the fuck?" She was never against me trying new things, but she hated it whenever I launched without a plan. Which, given how I got here in the first place, I could understand.

Spinning my wheels in gravel is a pretty good metaphor for how I felt. I had already spent a week—half of my outpatient time—in the new therapy gym and I hadn't met a single goal. I couldn't even take pills by myself yet. I was losing patience and giving in to my restless, competitive self again. I felt angry and anxious. Time was running out. All week I had worked full throttle without taking any time off.

After the weekend, I poured everything into sitting up and getting dressed. The combination of the previous week's intense work and a much-needed Sunday rest had paid off somewhat. I was able to stay up a little longer, but it wasn't enough. I couldn't try any harder. I pulled so hard in my effort to sit up that I almost tore my biceps.

My therapy team was working hard, but I found myself getting really tired of failing under their watchful eyes. Annoyed, really. Ever since I was a kid, I hated having people watch me struggle. In sports, I always wanted to dominate, and I mostly did. The competitor in me didn't want to be less than the best. That's one reason I put so much effort into athletics and spent all those late nights shooting lacrosse balls in the yard or watching game film. That goes back as far as I can remember. When I had a hard time with things, I preferred to disappear someplace where I could figure it out on my own.

Now I'd been struggling for twelve weeks with people watching every little failure. Every big failure too. Their eyes on me as I tried to put clothes on, tried to roll over, tried to prop sit, tried to use a manual chair, tried to roll through a shopping mall without freaking out.

At this point, all I wanted was to hear some instruction and then go hide in my apartment and try a thousand more times to put on my damn clothes like a normal person.

At the beginning of 2013, I was an athlete at the top of his game. Three months later I was about to return home from a rehabilitation hospital still unable to do a damn thing. I wasn't used to struggling, and being a failure like this was so hard to comprehend.

There were so few days left and so much undone and so many people waiting at home to see how I'd changed. All those eyes.

I couldn't help thinking about a former patient who strolled into the adolescent gym one day while I was still in the inpatient program. He told me that he had stayed in Room 430, too, and that it was a good omen for me. Before he left inpatient, he had started to walk again, and he was sure that I would too. At the time it gave me a little boost, but now it just seemed cruel.

Thanks, dude.

═══════════════════

I'm paralyzed. I can't move. Things really haven't gotten much better. This is so much harder than I thought it would be. This is so much harder than I thought. This is so much harder than I thought. This is SO. MUCH. FUCKING. harder than I thought it would be. FUCK. I don't know if I can do this anymore.

I was starting to freak out.

I stayed awake many of the last nights in Atlanta thinking and thinking. Luckily I had a view out the window right next to the bed, and on those final nights the Georgia moon was kind enough to visit. I liked having something that wasn't me or my future to stare at.

Who was I and where was I? I was on the outside at Shepherd yet still a part of the hospital. I felt sort of born again here, but not yet fully born. As much as I wanted to go back north, I couldn't envision myself in a place other than the hospital. Or I was afraid to. I was close to going home but felt disconnected from my Tyngsboro life. No, not disconnected, but different.

Afraid, mostly, of the future but trying to stay in the moment. But which was harder to accept? Right now I was still flopping uselessly around in bed or motoring around in a special chair. Was that my future, or would there be some magical improvement that I hadn't seen here? I was so young, and there were so many years ahead of me. What kind of trip was it going to be? I thought a lot about my friends and what they would think about all of it.

But that was the problem. Other than my parents, especially my mom, nobody really had any idea of what I was doing or what I looked like. The crowd at the fundraiser only got a glimpse of me on the screen. Outside of family, hardly anyone visited me in Atlanta. All the people I was going home to only had their imaginations to work from. If they were thinking about me at all. I mean, I talked to some people through text messages and Skype, but I felt like I'd been away from them for so long. It was only a few months, but it still felt like I'd been away for a lifetime.

Which meant that it felt like forever to them too.

Who was I in their imagination? The old healthy Jack? Some new different Jack they weren't sure they wanted to deal with? The old Jack who got injured and who had tens of thousands of dollars raised for him so he could get healed and come back totally healthy?

Really, I kind of wished people saw me in the early months of Atlanta so they knew everything I'd gone through to get to where I was now.

Nobody saw me at my worst time. They could imagine all they wanted, but they really couldn't understand what it was like before I could lift my arm to scratch my nose. Before I could sit upright without passing out. Before I got rid of the neck brace, the mobile arm support, and the splints on my useless wrists. Nobody saw any of it.

Except for my family, nobody, not even Justin and Derek, saw me struggling and fighting every day. Nobody saw how the mental battle was even harder than the physical one. No one, not even Mom, was inside my head as I wrestled with the fact that I was paralyzed.

It's hard, especially as a kid or adult or whatever I am, to have to accept it. But I had to deal with it. I was an athlete who may never play another down or score another goal. As dark as that is, it's all I could think about some nights.

Not only was I scared of the distant future, but I had to worry about the next day and how I would overcome all the obstacles that came with it. And then go through another long night and do it all again.

I was downright scared. Contrary to the image I liked to put out to everyone, I was afraid of what had happened to me and I was afraid of being talked about when I got home. People asking: What happened to that guy? Is he going to get better? Why isn't he better yet? I didn't want to answer these questions.

Actually, I didn't want to admit that I *couldn't* answer some of those questions.

Every now and then while lying in the dark I said to myself quietly, "I'm really in a wheelchair," or, "I can't move." Each time it hit me like a shock. Fear and anxiety had become frequent companions. I realized that I was becoming a more anxious person.

I was still so new to everything. I was only at the beginning of dealing with an injury that took years to truly adapt to.

And I had plenty of years ahead of me.

My age was a good news, bad news thing. Yes, I had been hit early and hard, but I was stronger and healing better than an older adult with the same injury.

I don't know, maybe an adult would be calmer while dealing with this? But I thought about my dad or mom having their C6 smashed like mine, and how hard that would be. It made me want to cry, actually.

It was hard enough knowing that my mom was in a bed nearby, sleeping off another difficult day in Atlanta, watching her son maybe/kinda/sorta recover from a traumatic SCI. For all I knew she was lying awake right then, too, thinking about this nightmare and its future.

I had the rest of my life to get better, and I would be damned if I didn't. I had to keep telling myself, and be told by others, that I was still a rookie. Maybe I couldn't see what would happen down the road because there were too many possible outcomes. Anything could happen, and I needed to take it one step at a time, so to speak, one useless foot in front of the other . . . I guess I thought about all this at nighttime because it was the only time when people weren't hovering around me, guiding me, giving me one lecture or another. It was the only time of day I had to myself, when I could actually have these thoughts. Having to perform for everyone as a patient and son, to be serious all the time, to be the optimistic victim of a tragic accident, it was so much to handle that sometimes it hit me like a train at night.

These nights were lonely in more ways than one. I wasn't telling anyone about them, or about the thoughts and fears that plagued me. There was no way I was going to talk to anyone, not my mom or dad and especially not a psychologist. I understood why some people do, and that makes sense to me too. Each of us should do what we think is right. Some problems are best worked out through conversation. Most of us have mental laundry that could use some airing out—talked through, sorted out—rather than left folded up and molding in some dark corner. But I felt like I had to handle things on my own.

That's how I've always been. I keep to myself, but if I have something to say, I'll say it. But not about this. Maybe it was denial, I don't know, or fear of admitting my fears. I didn't want to say out loud those things I whispered in the darkness to myself. It probably—no, definitely—made my life harder, but I wanted to quarterback my own game, and I didn't want a coach getting inside my head. I knew I'd have to take some hits.

I don't know the source of my refusal. It's been with me as long as I can remember. It's the way I dealt with things, and I wasn't going to change, especially if somebody told me to. Call me stubborn and you'd be right. If it meant having more long dark nights like these, then so be it. I was surviving. I figured it was on me to deal with the crappy cards I had been dealt and to win the game if I could.

At least in the middle of the night I wasn't asking, "Why me, Lord?" or at least not very much. I figured I had my place in this world and that's the way it goes. Shit happens to some people, and I was one of those people. So the question for me wasn't so much "Why me?" as "Now what?" That was my philosophy, or as much philosophy as I had at seventeen.

Speaking of philosophy, "everything happens for a reason" was playing through my head on a loop. It's such a powerful sound bite. I wanted to believe it, because it sort of wrapped up the mystery of "What the hell just happened to me?" in a nice little package. But it's so weird to be comforted by the suggestion that so much sadness and cruelty is part of "God's plan." One look at the kids in wheelchairs at the Shepherd Center, or a glimpse into the darkened hall of the TBI unit, and you have to wonder what the hell kind of plan we're part of.

I mean, there are so many valuable lessons to learn here, about patience, kindness, devotion to others, resilience, and compassion. But it was easier to wrap my head around the idea that patients, families, and staff were all simply dealing with tragic accidents than the idea that everything was happening for a reason.

I don't know. But I knew that I was changing, becoming more serious. You can't spend night after night dealing with so much drama and trauma without changing. My body had been altered, and now my mind was transforming too. A new journey had begun, inside and out.

I know I talk a lot about the "new Jack" and about being kind of reborn through this accident, and yes, I grew up going to church until my parents divorced, and yes, I couldn't help but pray to God to help me out of this mess, but I don't mean that I was reborn in any spiritual way. I just mean my life was turned upside down and I had to reimagine how to live.

If anything, all the work and suffering I was doing made me think more about self-reliance than benefitting from a helpful Lord. My dad kept reminding me in his loving way about the importance of devotion: "You're good, you're strong, and you're smart. Say your prayers."

He was sure that devotion would help see me through, and so I prayed, but I couldn't help but feel that the path forward was built mostly by the other stuff he emphasized: hard work, a loving family, and a supportive community.

If you're good, strong, and smart, why are you asking for favors from God?

During my inpatient experience there were people from a church who came by once in a while and asked if I wanted them to say a prayer or if I wanted to attend a service. Other than the prayer, I declined. Generally, I prayed alone, and anyway I couldn't feel as connected to these people of faith as I was to Patty and Cathi and the nurses. I won't say that doing assisted push-ups while insulting the Yankees was like church for me, but I will say that the first wisdom and grace that came my way after the accident was the result of hard work, not prayer.

And I learned a lot on these dark nights too. I was freaking out and watching myself freak out. I was working through things and watching myself work through them. I was unhappy and anxious, and I was coping with sadness and anxiety. It was an exhausting lesson in resilience.

I was awake most nights, but somehow had the energy to make it through the next day. I woke up, got my shit together, and passed through the parking garage to the main building just like every other day. I worked hard right up to the end. I was not lazy. Another few days to go, and then I was homebound. My goals from the first week carried into the second, but there wasn't enough time to complete anything.

I made a few trips up to the fourth floor to say hi and bye to Patty and Cathi and Cheryl, and they were always happy to see me. They encouraged me as they always had, but it felt different. I wasn't their client anymore. They had a full roster of new SCI cases to look after, and I was increasingly in the new and strange role of former patient. To be honest, it felt a bit lonely.

The outpatient period had been more of a brief reality check than a chance to make real progress. A week or two is nothing in this new life. I was learning how to handle myself and realizing— again—that I needed patience.

There had been no improvement in managing my blood pressure or body temperature. The spasticity had increased, and we were treating it with medication. I still couldn't do much in the manual chair. I needed help with medication and transportation. I needed help from my parents. I relied on doctors and nurses to keep me alive. I had a long road ahead of me doing PT, OT, and strength training.

There is always going to be struggle, and there will always be people watching.

At least I knew exactly what I had to work on at home: everything.

It was a hell of a lot of homework—a lifetime's worth, maybe— and once I started therapy in Boston I could pick up where I left off.

It was time to pack my things and head home. Really, I wanted to stay at the Shepherd Center until I accomplished a lot more. I mean, why go home if I haven't reached my goals and if I won't make as much progress there? Could I survive on my own without the constant attention of people like Patty and Cathi?

But my time in Atlanta had run out. Insurance wouldn't cover the rehab much longer, and Mom needed to get back to work. She'd left the day I was injured and hadn't been back for three and a half months. And I had to return to school soon if I wanted to graduate on time.

I was excited to go home, but I was nervous as hell about it. I felt like being home would bring some clarity to the chaos, but I wasn't sure I'd like what I saw. Could I live in my house? How were people going to treat me? How would I handle school?

I knew people would be cheering for me, but cheering can only do so much. And like any football game, eventually the cheering stops and people go home.

I was going back to real life, a very real and very different life.

9

THE LITTLE THINGS

People passing by; stories passing by. I never understood it before, but I get it now. I can see that people have stories inside them in the same way I feel my stories spinning around inside me.

I woke up early that morning. Or maybe I'd never fallen asleep. I couldn't really tell the difference anymore. All I could think about was going home.

April 27, 2013. It was exactly one hundred days since the accident. The day already felt momentous, but it was weird how a big round number made it seem bigger.

As I lay in bed, I could feel myself being stretched thin between two feelings. I desperately wanted to race to the airport and fly back to Boston, and I desperately wanted to stay right where I was until I was stronger and more mobile. These people—Cathi, Patty, and the others—had totally changed my life. If I stayed for weeks or months more, what else could their expertise and the Shepherd Center's facilities do for me? What was I giving up by leaving?

It was FOMO—fear of missing out—but in both directions and at maximum strength. All the friends and family I was missing at home versus all the training and recovery I would miss when I left Atlanta.

Before I knew it Mom and I were at Hartsfield-Jackson Airport with tickets for a nonstop flight to Logan Airport. I was cold as usual, but I also had cold feet. I wanted to run back to the safety of the Shepherd Center. We were really on our own now. Of course we had the Shepherd staff on call if we had questions, but a phone call is nothing compared to living in the facility.

My story had entered its next chapter. And so, I could only look forward. I was filled with anticipation, with an impatience that made me want to skip right to the end of the chapter so I could see how it all turns out when I returned to my family, friends, and hometown.

First, though, I had to meditate for a while at the mini-Dunkin' Donuts in the airport. Our flight wasn't leaving for a while, and I wanted to stuff some calories in my face, and I liked the fact that Dunkin' is a chain that started in Boston. It was like a fairy tale where I followed the trail of glazed donut crumbs back to my home.

Really, though, I was people-watching and thinking about everything I had gone through. Now that I had finally left the Shepherd Center bubble, I could see more clearly what had happened. I just spent three months at an intense rehab facility two thousand miles from home. My family and I had made a decision to upend our lives and go into the unknown with the hope that it was the best decision for my recovery.

My time in Georgia seemed like a strange and intense dream. There was still a tiny part of me that felt like I might wake up at any moment to find life was all back to normal. I would still be the old Jack. But you know that whole mind-bending *Inception* question about whether reality is any more real than a dream? My time at the Shepherd Center also felt like the most real thing I had ever done, more real than the teenage life I'd been living in Tyngsboro, more real even than the best moments of my short football career.

It's not like I left home to spend time on the beach or go out to eat. I was in the therapy gym six days a week working on the little things in order to get better. And by the little things I really mean little things, like trying to scratch my face or roll onto my stomach. The little things that helped me get back to living a normal life and doing the things I love. The little things able-bodied people all take for granted. The little things that make life real. Because little things are often the biggest things.

Life at home now seemed like a dream, especially the life I'd led before. The life I had ahead of me would barely resemble what it was just 101 days ago.

For a moment I could see myself in the wheelchair from the perspective of the people walking by to catch their flights. If they even noticed me, they'd see a young guy with skinny arms in a chair with some kind of backstory that they'd never know. I imagined them wondering: *Was he born that way? Did he have an accident? Will he get better?* Or maybe they simply thought, *Sucks to be him.* In my mind I felt like I stood out, both because I was in the chair and because I had this crazy secret story.

But then I realized that every one of them had their own secret stories too. Everyone has their own tale to tell. Everyone is suffering or has suffered or will suffer some kind of terrible loss. Everyone in the airport, like in life, was on their own journey.

Maybe it's a cliché, I know, but it still hit me hard. There is so much going on inside each person who crosses our path, but we don't see it. I hadn't really understood it before, maybe because until now I didn't have that much going on inside me. Everything I'd gone through since the accident suddenly opened up a door into understanding what others might be going through.

It's not like I hadn't heard the words *compassion* or *empathy* before, but it felt like now I could live inside the words for the first time.

Then I started to think about the people back home. All the people who stood behind me in my time of need. The people who dropped what they were doing in order to help me. And suddenly I could really *feel* that there are such good people in the world who do care and who want nothing more than for me to succeed. Suddenly I wanted to go home to talk to people face-to-face. I wanted to thank them for what they'd done. I wanted to hear them speak.

In that moment I realized that my injury had not only changed my physical appearance but also forced me to grow up emotionally. I had a long way to go, but I knew enough now to think a little more deeply about caring for others and how others had cared about me.

I won't say that I realized the meaning of life while sitting in an airport Dunkin' Donuts, but I do feel like I came pretty damn close. I knew, as it was time to board our flight, that I would always remember this moment in the airport. It was one of those situations in which you wake up to a new reality.

The meaning of life, I realized, would always smell like coffee and donuts.

Dropping back to pass during the Thanksgiving Day game in 2012

Hitting a feature in the terrain park at Nashoba

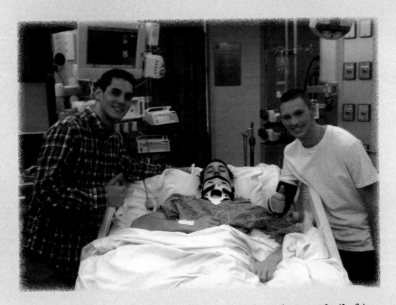

Photo at Boston Children's Hospital with Derek (left),
and Justin (right)

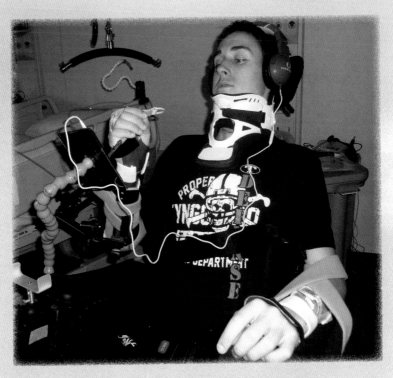

Photo early on at The Shepherd Center

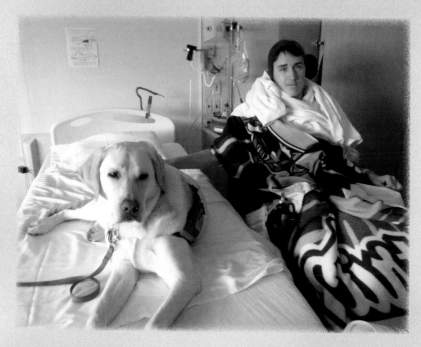

Pictured with Frosty the therapy dog at The Shepherd Center

Jack with Travis Roy in Travis's apartment in Boston

Jack with Paul (left), and Eric (right) on graduation night in 2014

First time using a sit-ski in 2015

Jack with family after finishing the Baystate Marathon

So this is what they mean when they say, "You can't step into the same river twice." Home is home, but home has changed. So much has changed. I don't know what to think.

A few hours later we landed in Boston. It was only two weeks after the Boston Marathon bombing, so security was really tight. Dad and Sam met us at baggage claim with open arms, then loaded me and our stuff into the car for the ride home. I was nervous but had a smile on my face as I watched the exit signs pass by one after the other. I couldn't stop thinking about that moment when we would pull into the driveway. I didn't even know what my house looked like anymore, how much it had been changed.

Exit 34 off Route 3, Tyngsboro, Massachusetts. I've never felt so relieved to get off the highway in my entire life. We lived a few miles away, so it only took five minutes to get home. My heart was beating out of my chest, and my mind was racing.

The experience of arriving was so surreal. I'd been thinking about it for so long. I peeked ahead through the trees to get a glimpse of my house as we came down Chestnut Road. There it was! My eyes lit up and scanned the place like radar. The exterior was still the same, an off-white split-level house with brown trim and four pillars on the front porch. It has a big overhanging addition in the back that my mom and dad had built ten years earlier. The detached garage hadn't changed either.

Unlike me, I realized, all the changes were on the inside.

It was quiet. I remember sitting in the passenger seat anxiously waiting while Dad got my chair out of the trunk. Sam went in through the front door and left it open. Suddenly at that moment

I wanted nothing more than to see my dog in the doorway, and to see his reaction when he saw me for the first time since January.

And just as Dad lifted me into the chair, there he was. Now he was looking at me, not moving a muscle. I shouted, "Bode!" His whole butt starting to wag along with his tail. Then he immediately sprinted right toward me, then around and around my chair in circles. I've never seen that dog run so much in my entire life. He was six years old but moving like a puppy again.

Other than when Sam put Bode in front of the camera during a Skype call, I hadn't seen him for a hundred days (which is almost two years in dog time). It was so nice to touch him and have him next to me again. After he finally calmed down it was time to go inside and see what a small army of people had been doing to my house since I left Boston.

My whole life I'd lived in an upstairs bedroom. Now I'd be living in a basement apartment. Since it was a split-level house, the basement could be accessed through a back door at ground level. I wheeled around the corner into the carport underneath our addition and found myself in front of a big glass door with my *Jack/7* logo right in the middle. That was cool.

Dad asked if I was ready. I said yes and went in.

And I stopped. What I saw stunned me. Nothing was the same. It was big and open, not cut up into small rooms. I felt like one of those spelunkers who crawls through a small hole and suddenly finds himself in a massive cavern. I expected an updated room or two, but instead found an empty apartment the length of my house.

I rolled directly into the living room where there was a big L-shaped couch, a table, and an entertainment center. We hooked a left into a huge central room with nothing in it except a counter mounted on the wall with a sink and a small fridge. I wheeled under the counter to check the height; it was perfect. The plan was to have a personal gym and desk in there, too, but for the moment it was like crossing a desert. What was weird was that the original windows were still in place, so I could imagine how it used to look even as I inhabited the future.

Beyond the middle room was a big accessible bathroom on the left and a bedroom on the right. Both were well-designed. The shower and sink and closets were all perfect. There was a Hoyer lift set up next to the bed. When the tour was done, I parked in the middle of the apartment to look around. The living room was yellow, the middle room was white, and the bedroom was blue.

I felt like I was in an episode of *Extreme Makeover: Home Edition*, but it was better than that because I knew that Mom and I had been taken care of while we were away. This had all been done for us. I didn't know what to say, so I hardly said anything except compliments on the quality of the work. And how I couldn't believe how much had been done in such a short time.

The best part of the transformation was an elevator donated by the Travis Roy Foundation. Travis, a Boston University alumnus and hockey player once destined for the NHL, injured his spinal cord only eleven seconds into his first game as a BU Terrier. Travis had since been confined to a wheelchair, but he transformed his life by creating a foundation to fund research and serve the needs of spinal cord injury victims. He wrote a book called *Eleven Seconds*, a memoir about his life post-injury.

Thanks to Travis, I could wheel myself into the elevator and go up one floor to my mom's living room and back to the life I used to live. Upstairs was home; downstairs was a blank slate where I could begin my new life.

All of this was made possible by a posse of hometown heroes. I had strong connections to nearly everyone who made all the magic happen.

Sam and my mom's friend, Melinda Baringer, lugged all the family stuff upstairs and decided what to organize and store and what to give away or throw away. Melinda and my mom met as ski instructors at Nashoba when Sam and I were really young, and they've been best friends ever since. Melinda has been there to support us since the accident.

Our neighbor, Dan Houston, is a police officer and was the main guy for the demolition. The original plan was to widen a few doorways and renovate the bathroom but that was quickly changed. Thinking ahead, everyone (except me) knew that I'd need more than a modified room or two. I was going to need a real apartment, built from scratch. So while a brand-new basement blueprint was drawn up, Dan and a crew of volunteers tore down the walls, ripped up the carpet that had been there since before I was born, and threw it all into a dumpster.

Ed Mierzwa was the contractor masterminding the whole project, and he was the first guy who knew I'd need a full apartment. He didn't want to do a half-assed remodel that would need to be redone in a few years. I'd played baseball with Ed's son Andrew since we were little kids. Ed and my dad coached our teams, and our families had been close ever since. Somehow as a busy contractor he was able to drop everything and spend countless hours at my house in the middle of winter to get this done.

Guy Denommee was the man behind all the plumbing work. Everything—sink, shower, toilet, baseboard heating—had to be torn out and replaced. I worked for Guy as a plumber's aide for the previous two summers, and I had learned a lot from him and his crew. I knew without looking that he had done excellent work.

The heating and cooling renovation was complicated because Guy needed to switch us over from oil heating to a gas system. Believe it or not, National Grid immediately sent out guys to dig a trench through the woods to a side street in order to tie into the gas lines. Normally they waited until spring, but they took it upon themselves to dig through the snow, frozen ground, and asphalt. It only took them a few short weeks for a job that usually takes much longer.

Nearly all the materials and labor were donated. Everything Guy did with the plumbing was free. Our electrician, Bill Wilson, rewired the entire basement, from lighting fixtures to power outlets, for free. Tile in the bathroom was donated by Joe Leal, who had been the head coach of my youth football team back in the seventh grade. Bob McClure, whose son Dylan was on my first football team, installed the hardwood flooring for free. Bob Engel, whose son Sean grew up playing baseball and football with me, donated two Panasonic high efficiency air conditioners. Scott Dillon and his son Scotty from Dillon Plastering donated their time. Scotty was a sophomore on my junior year football team.

You could pretty much trace my entire sports career through the people who dropped everything to make sure I would be safe and comfortable.

Dad was right at the center of all this, of course. When he wasn't visiting me in Atlanta, he was working on the house. This meant spending a lot of time away from his girlfriend, Kim Olney, and their home in the neighboring town of Chelmsford. Sometimes the people directly affected by a crisis need someone they can lean on to help them heal, and Kim was that person for my dad. She was his rock, and from day one she was in my corner.

Kim's son Ryan and I met on a Pop Warner football team when I was in the third grade. On the weekends I spent with my dad, Ryan and I always did stuff together, whether it was playing Xbox or riding mountain bikes. He was both friend and family. After my accident he brought a huge load of my *Jack/7* T-shirts to his school, Chelmsford High, and sold them all. Then he adopted my number 7 for his senior lacrosse season.

So I had an amazing support team while I was away. Everyone worked late nights and early mornings and weekends during the cold winter months. And it was a snowy winter that year, with one February blizzard alone dropping almost two and a half feet of snow. Nothing stopped them from completing a difficult, high-quality job before Mom and I came home.

But now that I've paid my respects to the people who made it possible, I have to say something else that was equally true. I was shocked at what I saw when I first rolled into the basement. One reason I didn't say much was because I was confused by how much it hurt to see what had been done.

Like me, the basement had been gutted, hollowed out, and changed forever.

What was once cluttered, familiar, and well-worn was now beautiful but bare, with almost nothing to indicate it was my home. The walls and shelves were painted but empty of pictures and posters, and there wasn't much else except some furniture scattered around.

In my excitement to return to a home transformed for my benefit, I hadn't realized that I wasn't ready for the transformation. I had never lived in another house. Other than the three months in Atlanta, I'd never left Tyngsboro for more than a week. So when I came back to the gift of a brand-new space, it was a blessing and a gut punch.

If they had stuck to the original plan and just widened a few doorways, then I could have lived with my fantasy that things had only changed a little. But like everything else I had dealt with since the accident, I had to face up to the actual scale of change. *Everything* was different.

It was going to take a while to adjust. At first I was only really comfortable upstairs where things were familiar. So that's where I hung out, eating and talking with Sam and my mom or friends and watching TV. What I really wanted to do was spend time in my old bedroom. But I couldn't. Ironically, it was filled with the remnants of the basement, which really were remnants of my past. It was so full of boxes and sports equipment and photo albums piled onto one another that I couldn't even get past the doorway.

How's that for a metaphor? It was impossible for me to reenter my childhood.

At the end of each day, I went down the elevator and rolled out into an empty place. I wanted it to be home, but it wasn't yet. It was designed perfectly for me, but it felt like I was in a hotel or some other kind of Limbo.

I spent the first night home in my new room lying awake and thinking about the day. In some ways it felt almost as traumatic, or at least as important, as the day of the accident. I had this hollow feeling that nothing would ever be the same, that my childhood was gone.

So be it, I thought. *Childhood is gone.* I guess I knew that already, but hadn't been willing to say it, or even think it. But now I knew. It was real, so I had to accept it.

---

*Good news: I'm back in school and the center of attention
again. Bad news: it's not because I'm the popular Tyngsboro quarterback. I'm on stage in front of the whole school
while they learn about my SCI. I feel exposed up here, but
it's not the worst thing. I'm finally reentering my life and
seeing all the kids I grew up with again. My story, and
my new reality, will get out to everyone at once. It's time
to do this.*

I was home. Home was different than I expected, and I was going
to have to deal with that, but it was still home.

There was a lot to figure out, but I had some time to do it.
I wouldn't go back to school until the end of May, when Patty
came north to give a presentation about my injury. I was looking
forward to seeing Patty and reentering school, but I didn't know
what to expect.

I had a lot of the month to myself. My mom went back to
work and I was almost always at home. PT hadn't started yet. On
sunny days, I rolled outside and soaked up the heat and watched
spring turn into summer. My friends visited after school and
on weekends.

Paul and Eric came by a couple days after I got home. It was
pretty crazy to see them for the first time since I was put into
the ambulance at Eric's place. I had exchanged a few texts and
messages with them while I was in Atlanta, but coming together
felt . . . well, I don't know exactly how it felt. I guess I'd call it bittersweet. I felt really good seeing them again, but it was mixed
with the sense of loss, of things never being the same.

The three of us shared a trauma that we'd never forget. My
story reached tens of thousands of people, but only the three of

us saw it happen. We were already tight—Paul had been one of my best friends since the first grade, and I had met Eric at the start of high school—but that day on Eric's hill made us tighter.

You'd think our reunion might have been a somber moment, but it wasn't. Maybe there were some nerves at first because life had gotten pretty real, but we were happy to see each other and be together. We didn't talk about the accident or look at the video. We weren't emotional. We didn't even treat it as a big moment. We'd had three months to process the accident, and by the time I came home we were ready to move on. We talked about school and friends. It was "What's next?" not "What happened?"

Which was cool, and exactly what I wanted.

Other than reunions, I was just existing. Which was weird after the high-energy days at Shepherd, but it was mostly peaceful. I felt some anxiety, usually at night when I lay down, thinking about the future and feeling trapped in my body. And even though the basement was stark and strange, a real bed in my own house was so much better than a hospital bed in a hospital room.

Spending time alone at home forced me to increase my independence. I started taking pills on my own—something that had always been a pain—because often there was nobody around to help. Every day, my mom opened the orange pill bottles and put together a shot glass of the pills I needed while she was away. She left a glass on the counter for noontime and another one for five p.m. All I had to do was roll up to the counter and grab the shot glass with two hands and throw it back like a cowboy in a saloon. I took three or four pills a shot.

If we forgot to set it up or if I needed extra pills, I went upstairs, found the box with the medication, grabbed a pill bottle, and bit through the child lock to get it open.

A new quadriplegic learns pretty quickly to use his mouth as a third hand.

Figuring stuff like this out made me feel like a new version of my old self. The little kid who snuck away to relentlessly shoot lacrosse balls until dark was now the older quadriplegic kid who managed his medications. As before, I never wanted to wait for help with anything. I always tried it myself first.

I worked tirelessly to figure out how to get what I needed without full use of my fingers. Opening a package of crackers was a hassle, so I became a raccoon, holding a plastic bag in my paws while tearing into it with my mouth. I learned pretty quickly which snacks were easier than others, and those became my favorites.

Of course there was still much in my life that required help and support. I could put on and take off a shirt or sweatshirt, but I still needed help dressing my lower body. I couldn't get out of bed on my own, so Mom or Sam used the Hoyer lift. Mom organized pills. Someone had to drive me around in the minivan. It would be a while until I learned to drive again. Part of me was afraid it might never happen.

My independence was limited, but that was the journey I was on. I'd work on making my body stronger, because a stronger body meant a more independent life.

Soon enough it was time for school. It was weird how much I was looking forward to it. I had missed four months of my junior year, and there were only a few weeks left before school was out for the summer. On May 31, I rolled my manual chair through the double doors into the main lobby where I was greeted by a huge WELCOME BACK JACK! sign on the catwalk, signed by everyone.

Patty's presentation was part of the Shepherd Center's No Obstacles program, which smooths a teen patient's reentry into life. The idea is to not only help me feel comfortable in school but also to make school feel comfortable with me. She asked me whether I wanted her to talk with teachers and nurses or with certain classes or to the whole school. I figured it was best to give everyone the story at the same time. That way maybe the kids I didn't know well might be less nervous about talking to me face-to-face or shaking my hand. My friends were fine, but I wanted to make it easier for the strangers too. I didn't need a bunch of kids getting weirded out by the one guy in the whole school with an SCI.

Patty also wanted to talk about injury prevention. The Shepherd Center is on a mission to reduce the number of accidents that lead to SCIs and traumatic brain injuries. The messages they put out there are pretty simple:

Jump, don't dive into the water.
Wear your seatbelt.
Wear a helmet.

In my case, I might add: don't build a crappy cannon box.

Patty's presentation was a twenty-minute PowerPoint. It was a quick version of what they taught me in my Atlanta classes: what the spinal cord is, how it works, what happens when the cord is injured, and how to live with SCIs. She explained the differences in symptoms between injuries at different levels. She talked about symptoms: autonomic dysreflexia, temperature regulation, and muscle spasms.

Like me before the accident, the students had some fuzzy idea about SCIs and paralysis. If Patty could erase enough of the mystery about what had happened when my C6 vertebra shattered, maybe I could reenter school as Jack the student, not Jack the strange tragedy.

I think when people know your story, they won't be judgmental or afraid to approach you. Like I figured out in the airport Dunkin' Donuts, we're all a collection of stories that connect us rather than divide us. The more we remember that, the fewer walls we have to put up.

The rest of the PowerPoint stressed that I was still the same guy I was before, if under different circumstances. She reminded students and staff to see me as normal, not different or "special." To do that, Patty had several key points:

If you can, sit down when you talk to me so we can see eye to eye.

If you're not sure about something, ask me. I will happily tell you.

Don't treat me any differently than you did before I got hurt.

If I need help, I will ask you for it.

I can still go to the activities that I used to go to, like the football games.

I am someone living with a disability. I am not crippled or handicapped.

I am a person first. My disability does not describe who I am.

For example: "That's Jack, he has a disability." *Not*, "That's Jack, he's the disabled kid."

Then, in her typical funny style, Patty said, "Jack's not brain-injured, or at least no worse than he was before . . . and he's not some fragile piece of glass that you guys need to give some kind of special treatment. Here, let me show you."

Before I knew what was happening, Patty quickly turned from my left side to face me and—thwap!—she lightly slapped me. I had no idea this was coming. Just as I started to show the surprise on my face—whap!—she did it again. We both started laughing—me at the shock of it, her at the look on my face—and then the crowd joined in.

Point made. I wasn't a china doll.

Patty was amazing. I will always credit her with bringing me back to life during my time at Shepherd. And I can never thank her enough for coming all the way to Tyngsboro to talk to the school, but did she really need to slap me?

For me, this whole show with Patty was as exciting as a rocket launch. It was a new beginning. For most of the kids, though, the excitement level ranged between "pretty interesting" to "Well, at least it's a half hour break from class." There weren't a lot of Qs in the Q and A period at the end of the talk.

I don't blame the students. It's my trauma, not theirs, and even Jesus would lose half his audience if he explained the Second Coming on PowerPoint. Most of the energy in the room came from the kids who crowded the stage afterward to say hi and catch up with me while everyone else shuffled toward the exits. It was the first time I'd seen a lot of my classmates, and I have to say it felt pretty good.

After snapping my neck in Eric's yard, dealing with the traumatic Boston surgery, putting in three months of hard work in faraway Atlanta, and hiding out for a month in my house, I was finally surrounded by the crowd who had been part of my everyday life in school before everything went to hell.

These were also the people who had sent texts, messaged me through Facebook, signed the quilt, helped raise funds, and put their name on the WELCOME BACK JACK! sign. Finally I was talking, laughing, and reconnecting with my friends and peers instead of just surviving alongside therapists, doctors, and parents.

Now it was time to figure out how to live my new life alongside them.

10

THE LONELY INJURY

Isn't it amazing what a little sunshine in springtime can do? I'm sitting outside with Derek and Justin, telling stories and letting warm sunlight wash away the hassles of life. In these moments I can feel myself growing like a plant. Life kinda sucks, but I can handle it. Good things happen too.

It turns out that the end of the school year was a lousy time to return. Everyone was distracted. In the last weeks of school, especially high school, all your classes and teachers start to feel like some kind of afterthought. I felt like I had stepped into the river of school right as it was speeding up and merging with the ocean of summer. It was a good test run for senior year, but it was an awkward time to rejoin the party.

Despite reconnecting with everyone, I couldn't help but feel isolated. In Atlanta I was part of a group of adolescents dealing with the complications of similar injuries. At Tyngsboro High I was the only one. No one else was going through what I was going through, nor had they ever gone through it before. Hardly anyone even *knew* someone in a wheelchair.

My sense of newfound independence was being tested to the extreme. I didn't have SCI-trained nurses I could call at any moment. What had been small issues in Atlanta could quickly become big ones.

But as dicey as my physical condition could be at times, when I talk about being tested, I'm mostly talking about the head game. My confidence and pride were taking some brutal hits.

Let's start with the fact that because I was the only chair-bound kid in the school, I stood out like a quadriplegic thumb.

Worse, I was much weaker than I wanted to be and was still unhappy that I hadn't met a lot of my goals before leaving Atlanta.

Even worse, I wasn't the confident athlete striding down the halls. I was the kid in the chair with atrophied legs and skinny arms.

And worst of all, I was no longer the popular Tyngsboro quarterback. I hate to admit it, but this is really what a lot of the hurt pride was about. I was no longer the guy who could lead the football team to an undefeated season. I would never again be the kid who was being hyped up by the crowd. I know how this sounds, but I don't know how else to say it. It's hard not to buy into your own hype.

We all struggle to figure out who we are, right? Well, it's pretty easy when the cheering crowd is doing it for you, and when the local paper and the coaches and your teammates and kids in the hallway are doing it for you. The problem was that I had always been introverted. School was a whirlwind of emotion and gossip. I never really thrived in social situations where I didn't know anybody or where I had to talk about myself. Until now I had a public identity given to me by my success in sports. I could just wear that label cheerfully.

Now everyone, including me, had to figure out who I was and where I fit in. I wasn't on top of the world. I wasn't on top of anything except the seat of my wheelchair. And it wasn't like I'd failed to score or lost some games. I was no longer the athlete I once was, and maybe would never be that person again.

Everything had changed. Everything. And I simply did not know how to process it.

I was never alone, and I always had people helping me out and offering me support, but the fact is that an SCI is a lonely injury.

I couldn't figure out my social status. I was part old Jack, part former star quarterback, part celebrity survivor, part second-class citizen in a wheelchair.

Thinking about myself at home was hard too. My life had changed, sure, but so had the lives of my family. I was constantly trying to figure out what was going through someone's mind when they were taking care of me. I couldn't help but feel like a burden, like I was somehow dragging Mom and Dad and Sam down and affecting them the same way that I had been affected. I saw my parents, siblings, and even some friends struggling to act happy around me sometimes, and I knew it was because they were thinking about me, about what life was like in my shoes. Obsessing about this wasn't healthy—the simple reality was that they were doing for me what I would do for them—but in a world where I required assistance every day it was hard not to feel the guilt and sadness.

My family had been strengthened by the accident, and I knew that I would be loved and looked after for the rest of my life, but that didn't mean for a second that being cared for like this was what I wanted.

But life isn't always about what you want, right? It's about what happens. And because of what happened, I needed help. Whether it was my sister putting on my shoes or my dad coming over on Saturdays to work out, I had to accept the new reality and try not to think about my time with family as sacrifices they were making for me. I'd go crazy if that's all it was.

The two solutions to this were acceptance and hard work. I had to accept the changes to my life but work like hell to do things on my own. That was my daily battle.

Thus, one thing I could do, I figured, was to stay out of the damn power chair. I didn't want anything to do with it. I was ready to do anything it took not to use it.

I was still struggling with my strength and didn't have the endurance to push the manual chair around for a whole day at school. I did it anyway. My arms were burned out and useless each time I got to class, but I didn't care.

Even though Tyngsboro High is pretty small, the hallways looked endless. Sometimes I'd ask Paul or Justin to give me a running shove down the hall and then hope I didn't crash into the lockers. Other than that, I never asked anyone to push me to class, and no one offered. It was pretty obvious I didn't want to lean on anyone too much. I tried my hardest not to look helpless.

Trips out in public in my power chair were rare, because I didn't want to be seen in it. The thing was huge and clunky, and the headrest made it seem like my entire body was bent out of shape. I was sure that it made me look more paralyzed than I actually was. And it was obvious that I was pretty seriously paralyzed. So why would I go out in public with a chair that made it look even worse?

I figured all I needed was a little more time to bulk up and then everything would be fine. Soon I would cruise around school under my own power and people would know how capable I really was. I imagined they were talking about me in the power chair, and I wanted that to stop.

The good news was that my classes went pretty well. I worked hard, but some of my higher grades might have come from the kindness of teachers who overlooked my missing the last four months of classes.

I was given every opportunity to succeed in the classroom. Teachers constantly asked me what I needed to make things easier. The main solution was to do my work online with an iPad. I could scan a worksheet and fill it out with a handwriting app, then email the file along with my other homework. Sometimes I felt like I had an advantage over other students because I hardly ever touched a piece of paper.

I wasn't a perfect student. Sometimes I was too tired to catch everything going on in class. I had limited ability to write things down quickly. The school did offer to provide an aide to take notes in class and write down answers during exams, but I declined. As always, I preferred to ask for help only if necessary. I wanted solutions that worked best for me, and to be honest, I didn't want to be seen with an aide all the time.

Though, an aide might have helped whenever I got stuck in the school elevator. I don't know if it was old or just moody, but the elevator had problems. One time it stopped at the second floor, but when the doors opened, I was about six inches below the floor. And there were times when I rolled in to go downstairs, the door shut, but the elevator didn't go anywhere. Eventually one of my friends—probably Justin—figured out that if they jumped up and down a couple times, they could kick-start it into gear. If I was alone, though, I was stuck. It's hard to jump in a chair.

I suppose I should have told someone that the elevator was a problem, because it was kind of annoying, but part of me kind of liked it. I wasn't *trying* to skip class, but I couldn't complain about missing one once in a while if there were technical difficulties.

I also missed some classes because I was in the nurse's office. Debbie Donohoe and Eileen Flynn looked after me when I came in for meds or if my blood pressure was low. We were in the struggle together, because dealing with my needs was a learning experience for them too. They had the usual workload that came with five hundred students, and now they had to deal with my SCI complications too. Debbie and Eileen were genuinely nice people, the kind of people you like to see each day. Which was good because I would be seeing them a lot during senior year.

But no one at school was more supportive than Ms. Craig. She was the business teacher for the entire high school, and I ended up taking every business class she offered. So we knew each other pretty well.

And Ms. Craig was my kind of person, too, a high-energy, kickass, no-bullshit kind of teacher who was a combination of Patty and Cathi. We had always liked each other, but we became closer, I think, because her mom has multiple sclerosis. Ms. Craig was the kind of crazy person who buys a pushcart-like contraption to put her mom in so that they can compete as a team in road races.

She's been in my corner since day one. Well, even before day one, actually. In early January, as I proudly showed her the video of my backflip, she looked right at me and said, "Jack, be careful!" A week later I was in the hospital with a shattered C6.

A few days after my surgery, when Ms. Craig found out I was at Boston Children's Hospital, she stopped in the middle of her class to let the students call me. It was the first time anyone other than family had talked to me since the accident.

Now that I was back, Ms. Craig took me under her wing. She was the first person to ask me if something was wrong or if I needed help. She saw right away that I didn't want anyone to see how difficult eating was for me, so she offered to let me and Justin stay in her room for lunch. After a few days, though, she convinced me that it was fine for me to go to the café. It was a big deal for me to get over that self-consciousness.

She offered the kind of support I liked best, the kind that comforted me but pushed me forward at the same time. She believed in me, but more importantly she helped me believe in myself. I really believe that having her class every day kept me sane.

Ms. Craig also knew when to bend the rules. A few days after the seniors had graduated, I was dropped off at school as usual, which meant I was stuck there until someone took me home. But most of the junior class was taking "a personal day," an option I didn't have because of my visits to the nurses. By noon, though, there was nothing left to do but sit in the cafeteria staring at my phone.

Of course, I was getting texts from Justin and Derek. I looked around the cafeteria, thought about how I was missing out on the all the fun, and I texted them both: "Get me out."

They'd have to squeeze me and the chair into Justin's small Infinity coupe. Whatever. We'd make it work. They cruised to school, snuck into the cafeteria, grabbed my chair, and zipped me through the halls, avoiding the administrative offices. Not to throw Ms. Craig under the bus, but it's possible she might have smiled and turned a blind eye when this great escape occurred.

Before long we were flying toward the parking lot as we laughed our asses off.

Derek muscled me into the car and buckled me in, but there was no way the manual chair would fit into the Infinity. After turning it in all directions, they finally popped the wheels off and folded the backrest down before jamming the chair into the back-seat as hard as they could. It was like Tetris mixed with wrestling.

Done.

Minutes later we were at my house, hanging around outside in the June sun. I just want to say for the record that these are the kind of friends you want when life gets kind of shitty. As my junior year was ending and my first summer as a quadriplegic was beginning, these guys went a long way toward helping me adjust to my new life.

═══════════════

I feel like God has called a hard count. My body is revved up with an energy I can't do anything about. It's the middle of the night and I should be asleep, but it feels like I'm jacked up on caffeine and tied down to the railroad tracks. Trapped, trapped, trapped. Am I going to spend my whole life feeling trapped?

I finally started back with physical therapy after school was over. Three days a week a PT visited me in my apartment and helped me work out with free weights and TheraBands. The best thing we did was put the electro-stim unit on my triceps while we were doing band work. I think it was pivotal for regaining so much function in my triceps. Without the stimulation I wasn't able to get a full range on the TheraBand. Once I plugged in I could rep out a few sets.

Before too long I decided to take matters into my own hands and push the limit on the stim unit. With help I taped the electrodes onto my triceps and sat through a three- to four-hour session with occasional twenty-minute breaks. It's pretty crazy to let a machine twitch your muscles for so long but it was worth it. By midsummer I was doing it every day.

As far as the PT goes, I was glad to be working out again, but it felt more like maintenance exercise than a path toward recovery. I worked hard each time, and while I wasn't getting any worse I sure as hell wasn't getting much better.

It felt different too. In Atlanta I was very close with my team of therapists. We worked together almost every day. The pace of my recovery was very slow, but I could feel the changes in my body as I grew stronger. And in Atlanta each trainer was an expert in their field. Now my PTs were good, but they weren't specialists. Our work together didn't compare with the therapy that I had received at the Shepherd Center. This wasn't a surprise, but it was still frustrating.

I knew there had to be something else out there that was more intense and more likely to get me back on my feet. For the moment, though, all I could do was work hard and keep my eyes open for better options.

As summer started, I found the biggest lift to my spirits was the house elevator. Being able to wheel into that thing and hit a button to ascend back into my old life really did wonders for me. What I really wanted to do, though, was hang out in my old bedroom. Lucky for me, I have an amazing sister. Sam made it happen.

Sam sorted through and cleaned out the mountain of stuff from the basement that had been piled into my room. It took her almost three weeks. It was hard to watch more of my childhood disappear, but I was still grateful.

Sam also cleaned the room, wiped down the furniture, and lit a scented candle to hide the stale teenager odor before I went in. I have to say it was probably the cleanest that room had been in seventeen years. I wasn't famous for being tidy.

I must have sat in that room for a solid hour without saying a word. I felt this really intense joy that's hard to describe. I spent seventeen years living in that room, and now I felt like two happy kids at the same time: the ten-year-old looking up at his blue sponge-painted walls covered with posters of the Bruins, Celtics, and Patriots, and the seventeen-year-old absorbing all the old memories. There was so much to look at and remember, like the Bat Signal painted by my Uncle Bob. My closet was filled with shoes, cleats, boots, baseball hats, jackets, and other miscellaneous sports stuff. I had a bit of a shock when I saw the clothes I was wearing when I had my accident, especially the jacket that had been slashed open by the EMTs.

Despite Sam's efforts, I could still smell my childhood. But I didn't mind at all. Sitting there was like bathing in the past, a time when nothing seemed to matter, when my biggest worry was whether I had enough money to buy the new Madden NFL video game.

I finally had to leave the room and come back to reality, but the Museum of Jack's Life was there when I needed it.

The room wasn't my only reconnection with childhood. I bought a cross necklace early that summer. Honestly it was more Dad's suggestion that I get one rather than my own idea, but I think we all wanted to believe there was a superpower that could heal my injury through prayer. Dad was more motivated by faith than I was, but I definitely wasn't afraid to pray for some miraculous intervention by God, even if I wasn't sure it made sense. I wanted it to, so I kept praying through the summer. At the time, the cross felt right. If nothing else, it was an emblem of peace, faith, and hope. It was the feeling of something, or someone, watching over me. Interestingly, I wasn't as interested in the Bible. There wasn't some specific verse I turned to for strength. I was more motivated to ask, in my own words, for some help. At least that way I felt like I was doing some of the work.

On those dark nights when prayer seemed like a good idea, I also began to experience what I could only call a physical anxiety. It was similar to when your mind races and gets caught up on fast-moving negative thoughts, but it was my body suddenly flooded with an energy I couldn't control.

You know how it sucks to go into MRI machines because you feel claustrophobic? Well, I live my life in the MRI machine, especially at night. My paralysis is intensified when I'm in bed—hard to move and no easy exit—and this physical anxiety always hit me in those moments.

It was a rush of adrenaline and claustrophobia at the same time. My heart pounded like a drum, and I desperately wanted to blow off steam, but I couldn't move. I was a sprinter trapped in concrete.

These attacks didn't start in my head. It wasn't a mental anxiety that got transferred to my body. I might be awake thinking about something fun or random, or I might be dead asleep, waking up with the sudden urge to run. And when you're paralyzed in bed and can't transfer to a chair on your own, you're in an awfully vulnerable position.

And that's how I felt: vulnerable.

I had to call my mom to get my ass out of bed with the Hoyer lift and into the chair. Then I'd drive around the basement just to get the feeling of motion, even if I wasn't moving my legs. Sometimes I'd head outside to speed around the driveway in the fresh air, even if it was after midnight.

Imagine being a mom in your bathrobe in the wee hours of the morning watching your teenage quadriplegic son drive his chair manically around the driveway. All the late nights she had to deal with; all the Jack stuff she had to worry about. It was endless. Yet she was always there when I needed her.

Of course, I was still dealing with regular old anxiety too. It's just a natural part of having an SCI, especially if you're a quadriplegic. Anxiety is a natural part of any life, I know, but being young and a stranger to your numb body can be its own special misery. The usual questions rattled around my brain: Will I ever get better? Will there be a cure? How will I live the rest of my life? What about a career, a relationship, a family?

I had been injured during an important transition period. My peers were applying to college and thinking about life after school. We were imagining our future in the weird mystery we call adulthood. But I had to put that on hold to deal with my injury. And I had no idea when I might get back to it or if anyone would be around to talk to when I was ready.

I could feel my life's path diverging from the road everyone else was on.

Or, more likely, I was staying right here at home.

My worst moment that summer happened in early July. It was so intense that I still think about it sometimes. Everything just came to a head, everything I had been through, all my fears and frustrations. In a sense, nothing really happened. But it was like being hit by a train.

I was home in my new space about to eat dinner with Sam

and Mom. Sam offered to pick up takeout for the three of us, and I ordered a burger. When she came home with everything, we sat downstairs at the white table in my living room. Sam helped me open up the burger wrapper, and I sat there for a minute, deciding how I'd pick it up. I was in a good mood, or at least I thought I was.

Despite all my OT in Atlanta, I was still in my infancy with picking things up, especially bigger things that could fall apart. Think about how much is going on with your hand (or hands) when you pick up a burger. The spread of your fingers, the pressure each one uses to hold the burger together, and the rotation of the wrists as you pick it up and move it toward your mouth. It's complicated, but you don't think about it. I had to think about it.

I should have thought about it a little more. My wrist movement had improved but my fingers were pretty useless. The new normal for my fingers was weak and bent but mobile. My main strategy was tenodesis, when I pull my wrist back to clench the fingers around whatever I'm picking up. But a burger is tricky, especially because it has slippery layers that can fall apart. The trick is to move slowly and be sure of your grip.

I just went for it. I grabbed the burger, raised it toward my mouth, but before I could take a bite the meat slipped out and fell onto the floor.

Something broke inside me at that moment, something huge and fragile that I didn't realize was there. I threw the rest of the burger down onto the plate and sat there feeling disbelief and rage surging inside me.

I can't even pick up a fucking burger! Even as I felt myself losing control, I knew all I could do was let the emotion run its course. I tried to keep it together, but one thought—*Is this going to be the rest of my life?*—started screaming and circling in my head.

The dam broke. I put my face in my hands and just started crying. I cried and cried. Not hysterically, but with a deep, endless sadness. For my fate. For my future.

Sam, not saying anything, sat there next to me while I cried. Mom kept an eye on us at first but knew Sam had the situation under control. Finally, I decided to go to bed. I skipped undressing and brushing my teeth and just wheeled into the bedroom where Sam hoisted me into bed and put a pillow between my knees. I couldn't stop crying, and didn't until I fell asleep. Sam sat in a chair next to me until she heard me finally quiet down and breathe easily. She never said a word. She knew me like that.

I spent my whole life fighting to be the best. I was incredibly competitive and hardworking, and it always paid off. I was *always* at the top of my game, whatever my game was. But what did winning mean now? Picking up a burger without dropping it and freaking out? Being a quadriplegic who can survive with the support of his sister and parents and nurses and trainers? Is that victory?

As a sports kid, I defined myself by my body and its abilities. Should I keep doing that? Should I define myself by something else instead, like my mind or emotions? Because right now it seems like my body—with its *dis*abilities—was defining me instead.

I mean, sure, I get to define myself no matter what. My goals, my ambitions, my discipline and drive to reach for the stars . . . but even metaphors are a problem now. Look at a quadriplegic and say crap like "Seize that opportunity!" and "Reach for the stars!" and "Stand up for what you believe in!" The English language is built around the assumption of a healthy body.

Was I still a glass-half-full kid? Sure, but empty or full, it was a pain in the ass to pick it up off the table.

And sometimes being a glass-half-full kid meant choosing to forget my injury and my supposed limitations. I was a kid in high school who still wanted to do stupid shit and be more than my new label. I had the same urge to be alive that I always had.

So at times that summer I found myself practicing what you might call a willful blindness. In life, sometimes forgetting is even more useful than remembering, and so sometimes I forgot that I couldn't or shouldn't do all sorts of things. I just wanted, like any kid, to move forward blindly through the best part of life, to screw around with my friends, to forget about the dark hours. Rightly or wrongly, I was determined to live my life as if I didn't have the injury.

This attitude had its downsides, like the afternoon at a friend's place when I got a call from the PT at my house asking where the hell I was. I felt pretty bad about that and had someone hustle me home.

But mostly this living with risk felt good and right, even when it was ridiculous. Like the times I decided to drive my power chair a mile or two down the road to neighborhood parties. I caught a lot of funny looks, which isn't surprising. Tyngsboro is a rural town with narrow roads winding through the woods. There's no shoulder, no sidewalk, no bike lane, and definitely no wheelchair lane.

A quadriplegic in the wild is a fish out of water. Think about it. When was the last time—or any time—you saw someone piloting their chair down a country road? With a chair you live in a pretty tight habitat of home, adapted vehicle, and public places with smooth sidewalks. But that's not me. I had parties to attend.

My chair goes a blazing seven miles per hour at top speed. A two-mile trip might take twenty minutes or so. And it's a really beautiful twenty minutes, I have to say. I had a breeze in my face that smelled like trees and lawns and barbecues and everything else that makes for a great summer in Massachusetts. And I was free of the van and the helpers. Maybe I wasn't Jack Kerouac, who grew up nearby in Lowell, but I was Jack Trottier and I was on the road.

The first few times I did it, I didn't warn my friends. I just showed up. Inevitably someone would look confused, and we'd have a version of this conversation:

"Hey, Jack! Who dropped you off?"

"No one. I just rode here."

They'd pause and look at me, then say, "Like in a car."

I'd say, "Like in my chair."

I'd usually get a head shake followed by, "You're crazy."

I wasn't totally crazy. I never rode home in the dark, but I liked leaving the party right as the sun was going down. It's nice to be just a little buzzed at sunset as you're cruising slowly down a country road. It's not drunk driving, I decided, if you're moving at walking speed. And anyway, I wasn't drunk.

Yes, I was partying with my friends, but I didn't drink much. I had to think about the trip home, but mostly I was always worried about bladder volume. There was no way I could deal with bladder issues away from home. A mixed drink gave me more bang for my buck than a beer, so that was my preferred poison. Either way, if I did decide to have a few drinks, I checked first with my sister to see if she could pick me up. That meant I could stay past sunset too.

Alcohol reduced the effectiveness of my blood pressure meds, so that was another reason to keep it light. I learned to mix in a little water and stretch out my drinks to keep my blood pressure from dropping too much.

Some of these summer parties had fifty or more people hanging out and pretty much everybody was drinking or smoking weed. I smoked a little, mostly when we were outside and someone offered it up. They call it peer pressure for a reason, I guess, but I didn't have a problem with it. It wasn't a regular habit, and I figured it was better for me than drinking. I think it even reduced my spasms a little bit.

Weed wasn't perfect, though. It sometimes made me a little paranoid. Not about social stuff, which is what most people mean when they talk about pot and paranoia, but about my body. Weed intensified my awareness of my paralysis. It made it more real, as in *Oh shit, I'm really paralyzed.* It might be hard to imagine, but being high and unable to move most of your body is kind of a mindfuck. I was already aware of my body, and I was trying to have fun at a party, so it wasn't a moment when I really needed to meditate on my disability.

Back home, my apartment became a place to hang out. Having company over the summer made it feel a little more like home. The living room was big with a big flat-screen TV and a bunch of seating on a couch running along two walls. We watched games, played poker, whatever.

Sometimes we didn't want to do the same old stuff. Maybe we wanted to drive around, or maybe go someplace random. It's that thing that teens can do so much better than adults: to go nowhere or be someplace without an agenda. We just go.

When we felt like driving around and I didn't want to look like a soccer mom in the minivan, my friends threw me into their cars and took off. We just left the chair behind. It felt good to be sitting in a regular seat. It gave me a feeling of normalcy, like I didn't need a chair or handicap van or hospital bed. I was a kid in a friend's car driving around without a care in the world.

Meanwhile, every time this happened, my mom would go looking for me and find my chair sitting empty in the driveway. She learned to laugh about it. She knew I needed to abandon it once in a while as a reminder that it was a tool I used, not a label that defined me. And she trusted me and my friends.

Then there were the times we looked around for the next adventure. I'm thinking especially of a night we came home to my place after a movie. It was around eleven thirty. As we got out of the van in my driveway there was a quiet moment and we all just looked at each other with the same thought: *That's it?* Which to me meant, *We can't do fun stuff anymore? Let's not let the chair get in the way of a good time.*

I asked, "Are you guys going home?" There was a brief silence and then someone smiled and said, "We don't have to." The obvious choice, we decided, was to drive to a soccer field, get high, and look up at the stars for a while. We spent a few hours sprawled out in the grass (them) or tilted way back in the chair (me), talking quietly, enjoying the moment, and wondering if we were the only life among all the stars we could see.

We weren't making trouble or hurting anything. On the surface it's the kind of story that gets some bad press—teens smoking pot late at night on public property!—but after everything I've been through, I'm less and less interested in the surface of things.

When it comes to my body, my life, and my friends, all I want to know is what's really happening. What's the deeper truth? Cut through the bullshit, the fear, the vanity, the gossip. Let's do what's real, and let's focus on what's true. Life, wherever it might be in the galaxy, is short.

When I think about that night, I don't think of it as "stupid shit" or even some little adventure. It was beautiful and simple. It was a moment in time. It was wholesome.

It was the kind of night I needed to put my burger back together.

11
PROGRESS

I'm back at football practice! God, it feels so good. I'm dressed in full gear, waiting on the sideline. The field in front of me is marked by the white lines that measure success and failure, and it's beautiful. I'm so ready.

But the coaches won't let me play. They keep saying I'm injured, that I'm not in shape yet. Which is crazy, because I can feel the strength and energy in my body. I can feel it!

Oh, right. Damn.

I just woke up.

Again. This dream again. It feels so good at first and then is so frustrating. I can taste the freedom, and then it disappears.

As summer slowly ticked away, it was time to get my ass in gear. I was ready for the next step in my recovery, and I was ready to get back to school. Most importantly, I was ready to reconnect with Tyngsboro football.

First up was the local summer passing league. Neighboring towns compete in seven-man two-hand-touch football twice a week for five weeks, two games each day. Passing league was a way for teams to warm up before the season and to teach the underclassmen the necessary skills without the worry of being crushed when they first put on the uniform.

Being a small D5 team surrounded by D1 schools, Tyngsboro was always the underdog. Last year, my first year starting as quarterback, we finished middle of the pack, which was pretty good. But this summer was a rebuilding year for our program. Not only had we had lost all last year's seniors, but only three of last year's juniors remained. And I was one of those three. We had a team full of inexperienced sophomores and juniors (and two new walk-on seniors), and we had a new QB in Dave Walker, a junior.

Dave was bigger than me, about six foot three, and had a stronger arm. I had faith in him and tried my best to teach him what I'd learned the year before, but like pretty much everyone on the team, he lacked game experience.

New players don't have a feel for the timing of a real play in a real game. Maybe my greatest strength in junior year was the chemistry I developed with Tommy and Chuckie and the rest of the guys. I knew where they were going to be on the field, and they pretty much knew what I was thinking. You need game time to develop that kind of chemistry.

Likewise, you need time to learn how to coach, and I can't say I was very good at it. I gave Dave tidbits: "On this play, throw early," or, "When this is happening, don't throw at all," or, "If a receiver is capped, then he isn't getting the ball." Running the ball myself had been one of my big tricks, but I couldn't give Dave too much advice on that yet, because passing league doesn't allow quarterbacks to run.

Anyway, we finished at the bottom of the pack. It was tough to watch, and not just because of the scores. I was finding it hard to adjust to my new position. I was a part of the team, but I was apart from the team. I wanted to play so badly I was even dreaming about it, but it was always one of those dreams where you never get what you want.

Luckily, as I was beginning to worry about the challenges of the 2013 football season, I started working out at an amazing facility in Canton called Journey Forward. JF uses intensive exercise-based therapy to help SCI patients regain strength and function.

Dan Cummings, the founder of Journey Forward, was nineteen years old when he broke his neck diving off a boat into shallow water. He was told by his doctors that he would never live independently or walk on his own. Dan wasn't satisfied with that answer. He spent a few years in the Boston area undergoing therapy but knew that his needs weren't being met, so he took the initiative to fly out to San Diego and become a client at Project Walk, an innovative exercise facility specializing in recovery from SCIs through vigorous repetition of able-body-like motions. It took Dan four years, but he walked out of Project Walk's doors not only standing on two feet but with a mission to bring the truth back home. He created Journey Forward to offer the same recovery strategy to SCI patients in the Boston area.

I knew this was the place I was looking for. I had heard Journey Forward's success stories, and I liked that they had a reputation for pushing hard to get results. It had been eight months since my injury, and I knew the quicker I started, the quicker I could improve.

But of course there was a catch. There always is. My workouts at Journey Forward weren't covered by insurance. In their wisdom, the insurance companies decided that Journey Forward was more like a gym than a medical facility, even though it was filled with injured patients receiving specialized rehabilitation treatment. The idea that Journey Forward is merely a place for exercising is about as dumb as saying Fenway Park is a restaurant selling hot dogs and beer. There's something bigger going on.

It was bizarre, and sad, that insurance covered a PT coming to my house to work with TheraBands but didn't cover a facility with a much more comprehensive and effective program.

The plan was to go twice a week, two hours at a time. At $100 per hour, this added up to $400 a week and $20,000 a year. On one hand, the decision was obvious. It was an opportunity to recover, a path toward positive change. But it was a huge financial hit. I knew Mom and Dad would spend every dime if it led to recovery, but we couldn't guarantee a miracle.

So once again we looked to Tyngsboro for support. We had enough funds remaining from the previous fundraiser to get me started, and Dad immediately started organizing another one. I signed up at Journey Forward in mid-August.

I didn't know what to expect, but I figured the best thing I could do was to go in with an open mind. But when I rolled through the automatic door for the first time, I thought, *Wait, this is a normal gym.* I was looking at total gyms, stationary bikes, medicine balls, free weights, lat pulldown machines, treadmills, and more. I got a brief introduction from the head specialist Mike Rollins, who moments later had his team unclip my seatbelt and two-man-lift me straight into my first activity.

It was like that for every activity afterward too. There was no turning back. I wasn't scared but was certainly surprised at their approach, which was more aggressive than anything I had experienced so far.

For months I had trained my body to move like a disabled person. Now Journey Forward was moving it as if I was able-bodied. The movements felt strange and familiar at the same time.

Regular physical therapy for SCI patients focuses on their strengths, teaching them to do the best they can with what's working. The Journey Forward technique focuses on full body recovery, which meant training my weak or unresponsive muscles too.

I can't quite describe the feeling when I looked over and saw my empty chair. Of course I saw it empty every day at home, but this was different. Mike and his staff were working to make the chair permanently empty. And that's an idea that hit me hard.

That damn chair was what people stared at when I rolled by. Now it was just sitting in the room, nobody in it, nobody looking at it. It was only a chair, but as soon as someone sat in it, it became a label, a cage.

I zoned back in only to realize that Mike was talking to me, but I hadn't heard a word he said.

Mike was explaining DNS (dynamic neuromuscular stabilization). DNS is hands-on manual therapy that stimulates muscles to improve motor function in a damaged nervous system. For example, I would try to move my legs on an exercise bike while a Journey Forward specialist physically did it for me. Eventually, if all went well, new nerve paths would be created to engage the muscles and the movements would become voluntary.

I remember thinking, *What the hell are we doing?* I couldn't understand how pretending to move would teach me to actually move, but that was exactly the plan. Mike said it could take hundreds of thousands of repetitions for something to click. By endlessly saying, "Hey, wake up!" I was reminding my body how to move, how to walk. I have to say I was skeptical while doing it for the first time, and even at the end of the day when I was tired and heading home. It was a lot to think about.

But I loved the philosophy of "not accepting" at Journey Forward. Under their roof, I was not accepting that I had to move and exercise like a disabled person. I was not accepting my current situation but was instead trying to push past it. No one knew if I could recover like Dan Cummings did. There were no promises other than that the intensive four hours per week would improve my conditioning and strength faster than anything I had done before.

I wasn't expecting miracles anymore. I was happy leaning into this new hardcore strategy for recovery. It was looking a lot like football practice, but with no off-season.

Meanwhile, I needed a strategy to mentally prepare me for the actual football season. In late August, a week before school, the Tyngsboro football program held its annual mini-camp. Mini-camp was a two-day intensive prep for the season. We voted to select three captains, and two of the choices—seniors Mike Wagner and Dave Bangura—made sense. Mike, a three-sport athlete, had led our football team in tackles as a junior and was a bronze medalist at the Massachusetts state wrestling tournament. He would call the plays on defense. Dave was another tough kid, someone who could get laid out on the field but still come back eager for the next play. He was a good slot receiver, and I remembered throwing up a prayer and seeing him haul it in with outstretched arms fifty yards downfield.

The third person selected to be captain—me—seemed a questionable choice.

I wasn't sure I wanted to be a captain. Well, I wanted to, but how much could I contribute? I'd miss a lot of our practices because of my rehab schedule. The team would really only see me at the games. Did I deserve to be a captain? Sure, my work as QB the past year had been a big success, but I felt like I was taking on an honorary title rather than a job to do.

It's like I said about shared experience being the key to a good team. If I wasn't going to be around much, and if I wasn't practicing and playing, was I offering enough to improve their performance? And then, on the selfish side, I knew that being captain wasn't the same as playing. It brought me close to the sport I loved but didn't bring me all the way.

My life had changed, and I had to accept that. I didn't have to accept the permanence of my disability—Journey Forward was teaching me that—but I did have to accept that things were different in this moment, and I had to live honestly in response to the difference. As things changed, I would change.

My senior year of high school started on a Tuesday. With the start of classes, I finally decided to stop worrying about whether I was in a power chair or a manual chair. It didn't matter. Both chairs carried the stigma of disability.

Of course it didn't change how people treated me. I realized how much mental and physical effort I'd wasted being stressed about trying to look "less disabled," whatever that means. But I also knew that worrying about the chair had been part of my adjustment back to life in Tyngsboro. I'd needed a little time eating in Ms. Craig's room before I was comfortable back in the school café, and I'd needed to learn to relax about how I looked in the power chair.

I took the energy I had put into pushing myself around

and used it for working out at Journey Forward and dealing with classes.

It helped that I loaded up on business classes for senior year. I was planning to go to college for business, but I also really enjoyed being in Ms. Craig's class. Her room was an oasis for me during the long school day when I was exhausted or overwhelmed. I'll even admit that sometimes I randomly popped into her classroom and sat there for fifteen minutes when I was supposed to be somewhere else. In exchange, I always put in extra effort to do well in her class because of how much she supported me. I owed it to her.

Classes were going well. I could tell that the work I was putting in meant I'd have solid grades, so it was nice not to have to stress about that. I was busy enough managing my health. Dealing with meds and low blood pressure and exhaustion and spasticity was interesting enough at home. At school, though, I had to really up my game and plan ahead.

A seven-hour school day might not seem like a marathon to most people, but there were days when that's exactly how it felt. I missed some classes and was late or had to leave early from many others. I tried hard to be a typical student, but there were times when I just couldn't.

Every other day or so I had some medical issue that sent me to the nurse's office. It was usually because I was feeling a little lightheaded or because I was in a fog from my medications. Debbie and Eileen were still rolling with the punches as far as how to treat my disability, but they had learned a lot at the end of my junior year. Now when I motored in, they gave me a look that said, "Is this serious or do you need a breather?" More often than not I needed a breather, which meant tilting my chair back for twenty minutes until my blood pressure came back up.

Eileen and Debbie already saw me once a day when I came in to take meds or use their bathroom. Hanging with the medical staff isn't exactly how a high school student wants to spend their senior year, but I was lucky to have them. Anything I needed, Debbie and Eileen got, and if they couldn't find it, they found someone who could. I'll never forget the effort they put in for me. There were no easy answers, and we had to figure it out together.

One thing they didn't have to try and solve was my spasticity. It had a mind of its own and got worse when I got back to school. On a bad day I might spasm ten times an hour. On good days, things might be calm enough—maybe only one spasm in an hour—for me to email a teacher without a twitch.

After a while I hardly noticed when it happened, but it weirded out some classmates. People gave me a look—You good?—when I got a big leg spasm and my knee bumped up against the table or my foot shot out with no warning.

There was no rhyme or reason to it. There was a twitchy neurology under my skin that no one could predict. Sometimes I thought of it as messed-up programming in a computer network. The flow of information between my body and my brain had been interrupted. The isolated nervous system was improvising because it no longer had me to do the thinking for it. The twitches, I figured, were really glitches.

I was also paying a price for no longer using the manual chair in school. My upper body wasn't working as hard, and my legs had been more constricted in the manual chair. So the twitches came more often and were more obvious. But so be it. It was a small price to pay for the benefits of the power chair.

I'm walking. I'm five foot ten inches tall again, and I'm looking you right in the eye.

A robot is doing the walking for me. No, this is not a dream. I'm along for the ride, but I'll take the robot over the chair any day.

Standing instead of sitting: the height difference isn't very much, but I feel like I'm on top of the world.

Dad and Kim put together the new fundraiser: The Jack Trottier Open Golf Tournament. It was held nearby at the Merrimack Valley Country Club in Methuen. The plan was to host it every year to pay my annual bill at Journey Forward. We made sure everyone knew that the funds were needed specifically for JF, and we put out a flyer on the tournament Facebook page with a story about my progress there and how important the facility was to my recovery goals. I didn't want it to seem like we were randomly asking for money.

The tournament committee—all family and friends—spreads the word as much as possible, and every year we end up with about 140 golfers on the links. Each tee is "sponsored" by multiple businesses, there's an auction and a raffle, and of course we have T-shirts to sell. And there's a big dinner at the end of the day for anyone who wants to be there and chip in. All in all, the day raises almost exactly what I need for a year at Journey Forward.

I love the committee that puts this together, and I'm grateful to all the people who show up, but having to raise money because of my disability is tough. I don't like riding the emotional roller coaster of guilt, indebtedness, gratitude, and humility. It's one thing to have an accident and afterward receive huge love and support from your community, but it's something else when the need for support looks like it might go on forever. I don't want to have to navigate all these emotions, but I do. That's part of my life now.

Every community is woven together. I see businesses with their *Jack/7* stickers in the window, or people in town wearing my shirts, or golfers I don't know out there on the fairways because they believe in helping a stranger in need, and I think about how we all benefit from each other. Even if I was a healthy Jack who had never been injured, I would still be part of a community of people who loved me, supported me, and provided services I used every day. Sometimes we don't think about or recognize how connected we are, but I see it all the time now. I have to. My accident pulled back the veil. It's not always easy to be the beneficiary of so much love, but it's still beautiful.

Thanks to all that community support, I was making serious progress at Journey Forward. It didn't happen overnight, though. My low blood pressure made it hard to sit up, much less work out on a machine. At first I could be upright for only a few seconds before I'd ask them to set me down and pick my feet up to return the blood to my brain. It took time to build resilience. But I did it, bit by bit, week by week.

As things became easier for me the specialists challenged me with higher intensity or a new task. I liked that they switched things around to keep it fresh and work my whole body in new ways. They always explained what we were doing and how I'd benefit from each exercise.

It took only a few visits before I amazed myself. I went into JF without the triceps strength to straighten either arm above my head, but suddenly I was doing a full push-up? I was capable of much faster improvement than I had realized.

Recovery is as much a mental game as a physical one. Maybe

the most important thing happening at Journey Forward was that I saw myself accomplishing things that gave me the kind of pride and ambition I had forgotten I could feel.

My upper body physical strength increased week by week, but nothing was happening with my legs. So, it was finally time to be introduced to Lisa Paicos, the Lokomat specialist. The Lokomat is basically a treadmill with attached robotic legs. I had been eyeing this machine for a few months and was anxiously awaiting my turn. They strapped my legs into the robot legs and my upper body into a harness to keep me upright. Once the treadmill was cranked up, I would walk with the robot's help.

Lisa smiled and asked me if I was ready to walk again. *God damn right I am*, I thought, but smiled back and simply said, "Yes." Groundbreaking. Even if I wasn't walking on my own, it looked like I was, and that was enough for me. It was the first time I had stood upright in eight months.

I looked directly at myself in the big mirror on the gym wall and couldn't help but smile. I was swinging my arms as I put one foot in front of the other. I looked like I did before the injury, when I was free to move about as I pleased. I knew it wasn't my muscles doing the work, but the image of myself walking was indescribable.

I hadn't taken a step since January, and now I was walking a quarter mile!

When it was time to come down, pretty much all my blood had settled into my legs. I was seconds away from passing out. Other than the usual brief moment of panic as I sank into oblivion, I didn't care at all. Low blood pressure? Whatever. I could have broken my arm and still kept smiling. I had just done something I thought I might never do for the rest of my life.

And I had looked Lisa directly in the eye as I walked in the

Lokomat. It had been eight months since that happened too. That's one thing no one thinks about in the litany of problems for an SCI patient: the loss of elevation. Why is it a big deal? Because height is status. We're not "standing tall" or "on top of the world." Down here in a wheelchair we're "low on the totem pole." Do you see, again, how language treats us? Low is bad: "bottom of the barrel," "underwhelming," "below the radar," and "beneath the notice" of able-bodied adults.

But watching the android Jack in the mirror walking into the future took away some of the sting and reminded me of how much was possible.

Meanwhile, I hoped that anything was possible for Tyngsboro football, too, but I knew that real success was unlikely. The first game of the season was on a Saturday afternoon at home, against Ayer-Shirley, and Dad drove me down to the school in the van. It was a quiet ride, with Dad giving me space to think. He knew I was wondering how the team would do without me, and wondering how the hell I was going to feel being stuck on the sidelines.

As we came around the back of the school from the parking lot and entered through the ticket gate, I got a lot of blank stares. People didn't know what to say. The local football die-hard fans hadn't seen me come down the path to the turf field in anything other than a football uniform. Now I was on wheels cutting through the crowd at waist level.

I saw a few hundred people sitting there ready for the game. And then it hit me. For the first time in my life, I realized what it's like to be in the crowd, to be a spectator. All my years playing sports I never really noticed them. They were just background noise to tune out as I focused on the next play.

I watched my team walk down from the school and then run

onto the field amidst the cheering crowd. I missed the hype. I missed the hours of butterflies in my stomach before the game and the nerves I felt while assessing the opponent on the other sideline.

I kept to myself while the memories from my days on the field came over me in waves.

I grew up with that field, spent hundreds of hours and countless games on that field. I was there when we switched over to artificial turf, and I was there when the old bleachers got torn down and replaced. I'd seen playoff games, big wins, and tough losses on that field. I had helped with youth mini camps and school events on that field. I have so many cherished memories that I couldn't forget them if I tried.

Was this the beginning of the end of my history with the field? Was it the start of a new history? Once again I'd just have to figure it out.

I went out for the coin toss with Mike and Dave. We stopped at midfield on the big red *T*. I had my back to the crowd but could feel the stares. Strangers who hadn't heard of me were asking what had happened or, "Why is there a kid in a wheelchair out there?" I couldn't get it off my mind, and I almost forgot why I was out at midfield in the first place.

The trip back to the sideline was hard. I couldn't face the crowd yet. I had to work through my self-consciousness. So I looked at the ground and watched as my wheels spit up the turf's little black rubber pellets.

Back on the sideline as the game kicked off, I couldn't help but wonder if I was more mascot than player. I wasn't participating or making quarterback decisions in the pocket. No one was cheering for me. I might never pick up another football, much less throw one downfield.

All I could do was help Dave evolve as quickly as possible. We talked after each series, good or bad, and we hashed out his missed opportunities. He took my advice, because he knew I had been in his shoes the year before. I knew I could expedite his learning process, and he knew he could take what I gave him and become his own type of player.

Somehow we squeaked by Ayer-Shirley and started off the season with a win. I had to smile, though, as I watched the younger guys celebrating. Experience on the football field and at the Shepherd Center and now at Journey Forward had taught me one thing really, really well. Victory, no matter how sweet, only lasts for one day. The season is long, and the challenge always lay ahead.

Sure enough, our next game was against Quabbin and they beat us pretty impressively, 32–14. Experience was the key, as they had a lot of returning starters who could put together a good spread offense. It was too much for our guys to handle.

I was even more impressed with the character of the coaches and players. For one thing, the Quabbin team had sent a card to me in Atlanta, signed by everyone. It's a measure of someone's character when they're willing to say, "Hey, that quarterback who beat us last year is hurt, and we should send him our respect and good wishes."

As with all the teams we played, we had a history with Quabbin. When we arrived at their field all the memories of a snowy November night game during my sophomore year came back to me. Playing a tough game under the lights and falling snow is something you don't forget. I was thinking about it as I traveled alone around the track to the visiting team bench while both teams were warming up. Soon, though, as kick-off neared, I saw the Quabbin players lining up and walking toward our bench.

I didn't understand at first that they were coming over to see me. I was by myself next to the bench as one by one the entire team and coaching staff came up to shake my hand. I fought back tears as they each said something positive to me. It's one thing to send a card, but when each kid individually connects with you it really means something. Quabbin was a class act, and I had nothing but respect for them.

So maybe I was wrong about a victory only lasting one day. Some victories, like when someone brings you to tears by saying a kind word or going out of their way to be respectful, can last forever. I certainly haven't forgotten what they did.

12

DILEMMAS

I'm back where I was nine months ago, lying on a Lowell hospital bed staring up at a blank ceiling. But now I'm a hospital veteran, not the scared rookie SCI patient I was in January.

To be honest, though, the fear is still there and being a veteran doesn't make it go away. Now it's more like PTSD than raw fear, but it's still real.

Before my injury I was really spontaneous. I was out and about constantly, and I'd change plans at the drop of a hat. Sometimes I was hanging out with the football guys, sometimes with Derek and Justin, and sometimes with some other group. I had several overlapping circles of friends, and I tried to be friendly with everybody. My relationship with each circle was a little different, but I was always myself. I liked being on the move and keeping my options open, sort of like a quarterback in the pocket.

Post-injury was different. I couldn't drive anymore, for one thing, and PT and medical appointments ate up a lot of my free time. So I slowed down and started to hang around with people I felt strongest about. I mean, of course I liked all my friends before the accident, but after a while I noticed that I was solidifying the truer friendships and not worrying as much about the acquaintances. I was still social, and I tried to live as normal a high school life as I could but when it came to friendships, I was choosing quality over quantity.

I honestly can't say how much of this change was normal for an older kid in high school and how much was because shit had gotten real in my life and, consciously or unconsciously, I wanted friendships that were just as real. Either way, I somehow realized that I didn't need a million friends, just a handful of good ones.

I had a tight group that I ate lunch with every day: Paul, Justin, Devon, Adam, Kyle, Monique. Most of my close friends both before and after the injury were guys, but Devon Milligan was one of the few girls that I grew closer with after the accident. As kids we'd always been friendly with each other. Devon had long blonde hair and a big smile. She was more extroverted than me, plus sweet and really smart. When you met her for the first time you felt like you'd known her your whole life. She's down-to-earth and easy to talk to, and since the accident she'd been there for me when I needed it most. Devon always looked past my injury and saw who I really was. I couldn't ask for anything better in a friend. At lunch and parties, it just felt good to talk with her and hang out.

Having a solid group of friends helped because in September I had started experiencing some intense anxiety attacks about once a month. They didn't seem to have a specific stimulus, but then again they often happened when I was in crowded areas, even sometimes in class. So maybe that had something to do with it.

It was more a realization than anything else, like how weed made things too real. But this was the paranoia without the high. The feeling came on slow, and then suddenly the only thing I could think about was, *Oh shit, I'm really paralyzed,* or, *I'm really the only one here in a chair.* Then I was hit with a barely controllable onslaught of thoughts obsessing on being trapped in my body or being the token disabled kid in the room.

Knowing anxiety wasn't uncommon in their clients, the Shepherd Center had prescribed Xanax for me before I left Atlanta. For a long time I hadn't bothered to fill the prescription. I had handled the long nights pretty well. But after the worst of the physical anxiety episodes and the first of these new mental anxiety attacks, I ordered up the Xanax. The drug almost always knocked the edge off within half an hour. Sometimes I couldn't wait and chewed the bitter pills to break them down more quickly. I'm not a fan of medications, and while I was glad I had the Xanax during the hardest moments, I eventually decided it was dangerous. I saw how powerful it was and how addictive it could be. After a while I decided never to use it again.

I was still dealing with the physical anxiety too. I was used to it, but it didn't feel normal. How the hell do you get used to feeling like a car stuck in neutral with the gas pedal pushed to the floor? I didn't know where it was coming from. Really I didn't even know if it was purely physical or partly psychological.

There was probably an overlap between the physical and mental anxieties, but it was hard to sort out. I was a paralyzed young athlete who feared that life was passing me by, so it was easy to understand that once in a while my body became frantic to move and my mind felt like freaking out. I've learned the mind-body connection is mysterious. It works both ways. A psychological frustration can impact your physical health, but a physical tweak can make you feel sad or frustrated too. What we think of as our mental state can actually be a symptom of our body being out of whack.

So once again I'd have to deal with the weirdness as it came, not knowing what was really going on but coping with it anyway.

Other medical problems were a little more obvious, though not necessarily any easier to deal with. One day about halfway through the football season, I came home after school and really wasn't feeling well. My blood pressure was abnormally low, and I didn't have an appetite. The severity of it increased as the evening went on. I could barely sit up straight even after taking my blood pressure medications and drinking a lot of water, a combination that normally evens it out quickly.

I faced my first dilemma of the night. Should I ride it out until my usual bedtime? If I went to bed early, I'd probably wake up at some ungodly hour and stare at the ceiling until six a.m. I decided to do it anyway. Of course I woke up around one or two in the morning, but it was worse than that. I felt like I was going to throw up.

Second dilemma: Do I wake my mom? We had set up an intercom system for situations like this. Well, actually, it was just a baby monitor, but I can barely bring myself to admit it because saying "I use a baby monitor" is like putting a knife directly into my self-esteem. The monitor is a useful, affordable piece of technology, and that should be all that matters. But the word "baby" sticks in my throat anyway.

I really didn't have a choice. I had to wake her. Without her help I was going to throw up on myself. So I called into the monitor for a few minutes until she woke and came downstairs. I threw up, she helped me out, I felt better, and we both tried to get back to sleep.

Then it happened again half an hour later. And again half an hour after that. And again. Each time I felt fine afterward, and each time the feeling came back. After the ninth or tenth time I knew I wasn't going to school and had to let the sickness run its course. The problem was that as a quadriplegic my immune system wasn't as good as it used to be. I had a hard time fighting off colds, flus, pneumonia, whatever, and it took me a long time to get over them too.

I was becoming dehydrated, I wasn't eating, and most importantly I was starting to skip my medications. If I miss even one of my many blood pressure meds, I can't sit up in my chair, which means I can't leave the house.

Which led to my third and biggest dilemma: Do I go to the hospital? As you might imagine, I *never* want to go into a hospital again. I dread it, especially if it means spending the night. I felt this way before my accident, and it got a thousand times worse afterward.

I can't stand the smell of saline and cleaning chemicals, and I can't stand the beeping machines. It all takes me back to the ICU in Boston. That was such an intensely traumatic time for me and my family. Whenever I'm back in a hospital I feel a bit of PTSD, and the fears I had in Boston come back to me: What the hell is going on? Am I going to die?

I grew up with an athlete's philosophy about pain, and I stick to it. If an injury doesn't require medical attention and doesn't pose a risk to your health, then rub some dirt on it and keep going. As I think about it now, this was only partly about me being tough.

The rest of it was me being totally anxious about hospitals.

I think that's why I took so long to ask for medical assistance on the day I broke my neck. Lying there in the snow I knew I'd probably have to spend the night if an ambulance came to get me. As a quarterback and snowboarder who got bumped and bruised a lot, I preferred to deal on my own with my injuries. Until I learned that it doesn't always work that way.

Some lessons are not learned easily, though. Against common sense I decided to wait out whatever had made me sick all night. My optimism that I would get better, and my fear and loathing of hospitals, pushed me to wait way too long. By three p.m. it had been eighteen hours since I last ate or drank anything, but more importantly I had missed three doses of my meds.

I was driving my mom crazy as I kept denying her attempts to call an ambulance. I was sure—or hoping—that each hour was the last. I had never been to the hospital merely because of sickness, and it wasn't a habit I wanted to get into. I waited one more hour, and at four p.m. my mom ignored me and made the call.

The EMTs arrived, asked the usual questions, and then put my feverish body on the gurney. I wasn't wearing a shirt, but the cold air felt good.

Fourth dilemma: How do I convince the doctors not to keep me overnight? I spent the entire ambulance ride determined not to stay in the Lowell hospital, even if it meant pretending to be healthy. I launched my plan as soon as the first nurse arrived to take my info. It wasn't her decision, of course, but I told her I "felt better" and that I should be able to leave really soon.

The doctor diagnosed it as the flu but said that for me the symptoms were increased tenfold. I should have been hearing "Danger!" as he was talking but instead I was thinking, *This sucks!*

So I stuck to the plan and put up a good front. The doctor said that if I went a few hours without throwing up and still felt better, he would let me leave. They gave me IV fluids and I told them I felt great, even though I didn't, and they let me go at eight p.m. This was tricky, though, because I had to leave in a manual chair, and I was hardly in shape to sit up straight, much less push myself around. Luckily Dad was there to handle it.

My escape was brief, though. The previous night's story repeated itself. No appetite, feeling lousy, tried to stay up but couldn't, went to bed too early, woke up at one a.m. feeling worse than ever, called Mom on the intercom, got sick every half hour until three a.m., then watched Mom call the EMTs again.

The same EMTs walked in like they had twelve hours earlier, asked the same questions, took me to the same hospital, and put me in the same room. Meanwhile, I had to decide if I was a stoic or an idiot. Either way, the doctors and nurses had me figured out and refused to let me go, even after a whole bunch of tests and some good sleep. By eight a.m. I felt perfectly fine—really—but they didn't believe me. I had to stare at the ceiling until two p.m., thinking about how embarrassing, annoying, frustrating, and smelly this whole episode had been.

And the final dilemma of this forty-eight hour saga: If I'm supposed to be growing up through this process of meeting life as a quadriplegic, what is the mature thing to do at times like this? Be a good, cautious patient and do what I'm told? Or be the strong, stoic guy who says, "If it's not killing you, don't worry about it?" Am I a smarter Jack who knows and admits the reality of his body, or am I the not-accepting Jack who pushes as hard as he ever did?

As long as I wasn't risking my life I figured I was more or less on the right track. There would be times when I'd be so ill that medical attention would be essential. I knew that. As I matured with my new body I would have to get better at figuring out when that was. I needed to be as unafraid of spending the night in the hospital as I was of saying "No thanks."

Likewise, my relationship with football had changed and I needed to figure out what it all meant. Some of our games took place a long way from home, so I had a lot of time to think in the van with Dad. Those trips were pretty quiet. I had a lot to think about.

I have played on a lot of sports teams, both winning teams and losing teams. Every team taught me that hard work was crucial, but each one also taught me something about how to be a good person and a good teammate.

For one thing, to be a good teammate you have to know your role. When Team Tyngsboro rallied behind me after my accident, my role was to get better. I had been trying my best and felt pretty good about my efforts to become healthier and stronger.

I wanted to do it for myself, too, but being pushed by a team really helped. I felt driven to succeed because of all the hard work done by my supporters.

It felt like a moral debt. People sacrificed for me, so I sacrificed for them.

We work our ass off in football practice for the same reason. We don't want to let our teammates down. I didn't want to let Tyngsboro down.

The biggest part of sports for me was always the camaraderie. I loved the locker room culture and hanging out with my friends. Pretty much all my friendships were founded in sports. And I think that's what made this football season so hard. That part of it was all gone.

I knew the team wanted me there, but I couldn't help but feel distant from the guys. I didn't enter or leave the stadium with the team, I didn't go to most of the team-building events, and as the season progressed, I didn't even get excited after a big win or feel upset after a tough loss. From my distance it seemed like all the games were the same.

I felt like a spectator, but it was harder than that too. Win or lose, I had the same numb feeling. I was losing what had been an essential part of who I was.

Of course it wasn't all bad news. For one thing, our young team managed to win nearly half their games, and in a few cases really controlled the game. We beat Clinton 35–8, South High School 42–18, and Worcester Tech 28–6. Some of the losses were just as bad, but Tyngsboro played hard and showed some heart. We knew it was going to be an uphill battle with the new squad, so I was proud of what they accomplished.

And on a personal note, Quabbin wasn't the only team to acknowledge what had happened to me. We had a game at Oakmont not long after my little hospital adventure. As I crossed the field, the coach and a few of the players came out to check in on me and wish me well. Oakmont is over an hour from Tyngsboro, so I was really surprised that the word had spread that far and that they still remembered me a year after our last game together. Small-town Massachusetts football is a community, and I was still part of it.

At Gardner, too, I was shown some kindness. It was wild to be back on their field and remembering our amazing win the year before, when at the last second of a hard-fought game, I threw that Hail Mary pass to Tom. This year would not be a repeat, though. We lost 14–0, and it was hard to see Tyngsboro go down scoreless. Gardner was still the tough team they had been last year, so I can't say it was a surprise.

After the game one of their coaches came over to talk to me. I could tell it was a personal visit by the look on his face. He approached me almost as if he knew me, which made sense once he explained that he had a good friend who was in a wheelchair. I think seeing me brought back some memories, and he wasn't afraid to really connect with me. There was no awkwardness, no hesitation, and no difference in how he looked at me or talked with me.

He asked, "How are you doing, Jack? How are you holding up?"

Without hesitation I replied, "Good. I'm fine, thank you."

He gave me a look that said, "I get it, I know something about how difficult it can be," and said quietly, "How are you really?"

He was giving me an opportunity to take down my wall of polite confidence. I didn't do it, though. I really appreciated him reaching out to me, but I wasn't up for a deeper, more honest conversation at that moment. I assured him, "No, I'm fine, honestly."

Of course the truth was I wasn't fine. Life was harder than I wanted it to be, and while good stuff was happening, there was no miraculous light at the end of the tunnel. I just didn't need him to hear all that right then. I'm sure he understood it already and understood why I didn't open up. I did feel better because of his act of kindness, and not only because his team had kicked our ass.

I wanted to be out on the field so badly I could taste it. But I couldn't, and that was that. Instead I got to help call the plays, with mixed results. Let's just say I'm not exactly Bill Belichick when it comes to making clutch decisions. A slow progression play isn't exactly a good call on third and two, for example. There were a lot of plays I later filed under "It seemed like a good idea at the time."

And I think I was starting to realize that the question mark of my relationship with football was going to be answered by coaching. Not that I would necessarily pursue a career in coaching, but that the challenge of teaching and advising and counseling these younger guys could be where I put all my football energy. I had to put it somewhere, because I wasn't going to walk away. And while it was an obvious answer—Can't play? Coach!—what I mean is that I had to embrace the idea of it. I had so much to learn, and it kept me involved with the game.

There was definitely a part of me that was excited to share my knowledge. I had planned to do it as a quarterback, but things changed. So be it.

I think that what interested me about coaching is also what made me write this book. Growing up through sports I had role models who shaped my thinking and reminded me of the kind of person I wanted to be. Sometimes it was my mom or dad, sometimes coaches, sometimes other players. Now I want to be a role model for younger players, and to whatever extent I can grow up to learn from my mistakes and pass on some wisdom, I want to be a role model in life too. I want to show people, in person and in this book, what hard work and determination can do even in the face of overwhelming odds.

I learned the hard way, over and over, to accept what I couldn't change even as I struggled to change what I could. I also learned that as the beneficiary of so much support, I needed to give back to the team whenever possible. I want people to know that while life's struggles are real—whatever their struggles are, and no matter how large—it's possible to push through and make meaning in your life.

And it's not only about the big stuff like work ethic and humility. It's about attention to detail. As a former quarterback *and* as a quadriplegic, I can tell you that the little things matter. Small changes in how you grip the football or recovering enough finger strength and dexterity to grab your own water bottle. You can do a *lot* with one finger.

Hell, I even wrote this book with one finger.

13

PURPOSE AND MEANING

I'm about to pass out, but that's good. I'm in the car with my mom heading home from Journey Forward. I've done this twice a week since August, but I still fall asleep every time.

No pain, no gain, right? It feels so damn good to be aching and tired. The weaker I feel after a workout, the stronger I know I'm becoming.

After football season, I started to relax somewhat. I had made it through the crucible and didn't have to be constantly comparing the highlight reel of my life with the consequences of my downfall. I had learned to focus on what was new and real—both the good and the bad—rather than obsess on my past. Football, at least the way I had always thought of it, was behind me. The journey forward was Journey Forward and college and everything else I needed to do to get better, stronger, and smarter.

Time began to open up for me for the first time since the accident. Every day wasn't some intense response to the paralysis or to the shock of coming home or to the responsibilities of football season. I was just living as the new Jack and dealing with all the ups and downs that came with it. I was living my story as it was now rewritten.

One of the funnier up-and-down moments of senior year happened in December. My friend Luke, who I've known since youth soccer when we sat together at halftime eating orange slices, offered to give me a ride to a friend's place. I was in my manual chair because I knew the house we were going to had some steps that the power chair couldn't handle. So I rolled into the van and locked my wheels as Luke strapped down both the front and back of the chair and clicked my seatbelt. We were good to go.

Or so we thought. It turned out that the front strap wasn't fully locked into the floor. The moment Luke stepped on the accelerator to pull out of the driveway, the chair tipped backward and I flipped over before I had time to say the *Oh shit!* I was thinking. Manual chairs have "wheelie bars" to prevent tipping over, but this was way too much force to resist. I landed hard on my back and hit my head on the van floor, which was padded only with a thin gray carpet. I was flung so far that my feet were still barely on the chair.

It happened so quickly that I didn't have time to grab anything, and Luke couldn't throw his hand out to stop me. Now he was panicking because there was no place to pull over, and he kept looking back and forth between the road and me on the floor.

Meanwhile I was looking up at the roof and hysterically laughing. The fall definitely got my attention, but it didn't faze me at all. I spent so much of my adolescence being hit harder than that.

It was the first time since the accident that I felt that kind of impact on my body. It hurt, sure, but it felt good, too. As weird as it sounds, I actually missed that feeling of falling and being knocked around. It's one of the things I had been craving all through football season. I missed being alive in a body taking risks on the field while trying to stay upright long enough to gain a few extra yards. Lying on the floor of the van, I felt the same surge of adrenaline.

Once I stopped laughing, I asked Luke to turn around and pull back into my driveway. It was an easy fix from there. As we headed out again for our friend's house, I made a mental note to plan ahead and know what I could grab if it ever happened again.

Otherwise, most of my adventures happened at Journey Forward, where I had progressed after a few weeks on the Lokomat to walking a full mile. The robot did the walking, so it wasn't the increased distance that mattered as much as my body's ability to keep my blood pressure up for longer periods of time. This improvement was the result of the endless repetitions not just on the Lokomat but with everything I did at JF. Repetition built up my stamina and allowed me, finally, to get rid of the goddamned ace bandages and tight knee-high socks that I had worn every day since the Shepherd Center.

I suddenly had the freedom to wear regular socks again. You don't realize how great normal socks really are until you are forced to wear those ugly compression socks day in and day out. Better yet, I could finally wear shorts and not have to worry about people wondering why my legs were all bandaged up.

Once again JF had given me a physical boost that helped me mentally. Anything that made me look less injured was a win in my book.

Months after beginning at JF I was still impressed every time

I arrived. As soon as I rolled into the building and said hi to the guys, I was also saying goodbye to the chair for the next two hours.

If I was starting with the stationary bike, they'd immediately lift me onto it, strap my gloves to the handlebars, and help me begin to pedal. I'd hold firmly onto the bars and watch my form in the mirror. It was always a kick to be up on the bike looking around. To be up there permanently was my motivation as I pushed hard and the JF specialists pushed me harder still.

While on the bike I had a trainer on either side of me moving my legs exactly how I would move them on my own. They told me which thigh muscles I should focus on as I tried to feel the movement we were making. When I started I also had two people there to catch me if I fell, but once I built up strength, that became unnecessary.

From there I might move onto the NuStep machine, which has a recumbent seat and lever-action handles for my arms. In no time I'd be sweating and breathing heavily as I pumped my arms and legs hard enough to hit that next personal best. Since August they had been timing me at one mile. I started out at nineteen minutes but by December had brought it down to fifteen minutes. I knew I could do better, and so did the specialists. They'd get enthusiastic and keep telling me my time as I dug deep for that extra ounce of power. Every time I finished on the NuStep they wrote my time with a dry erase pen on the mirrored wall in front of me.

For the first several months the trainers really pushed me verbally—stuff like "Push, Jack!" or "Go, go, go!"—but after a while they figured out that I had the work ethic to push myself. Every once in a while I needed a kick in the ass, but mostly they offered quieter encouragement and positivity.

I really liked that the goals at Journey Forward were more

like athletic training than regular PT. No one was patting me on the head and congratulating me for low-stakes accomplishments.

When I told the JF crew that I wanted to become strong enough to train for a bike race on the NuStep, they geared our workouts to that goal. When I told them I hoped to someday compete in adaptive sports outdoors, they structured my routine to increase my capacity to ride a manual hand bike. (A hand bike is just what it sounds like: a bike powered by arms instead of legs.)

More and more, I thought of my ambitions as normal athletic training goals rather than goals against paralysis. What I mean is that I wasn't thinking like a quadriplegic training in a special category. I was setting goals that made me feel like I had no limits. There are some amazing quad athletes out there now, but at the time they were rare. As far as I knew there weren't too many people like me training for bike races.

After the NuStep I might move to the floor for some push-ups, use a VersaClimber (with assistance), or get into a standing frame to shoot a volleyball into a Fisher-Price basketball hoop for fifteen minutes. Sounds odd, I know, but having to stand (braced by the frame) for that long while taking shots requires a lot of core strength. Another tool for building that core strength and improving my body's overall conditioning is the Power Plate, which is a vibrating platform I stand on while being spotted by a couple trainers. I hold onto a bar at waist height while my whole body is engaged trying to stay steady for several minutes at a time. After a few sets I'd move on to the next challenge.

If it was a strength exercise, I might be strapping my hands onto some cables or I might be lying down for a skull crusher. The skull crusher is a bar—actually a five-pound wooden dowel—I hold straight above me, but instead of moving it up and down like a bench press, I work my triceps by keeping my elbows up and lowering the bar toward my face and raising it again. My hands are strapped to the bar, but I needed to keep the bar from landing on my face. By the end of December, I was lifting the bar against gravity with their help. The next goal was to bulk up so I could lift the bar without help and eventually add some weight.

When I say "bulk up" I mean relative to my condition. Even as I improved and grew stronger and bigger, it wasn't on the scale of an able-bodied athlete. I was still thin. My SCI, so far at least, keeps me from fully developing muscles in the affected parts of my body.

Whatever my final task was for the day, I finished the final rep and then collapsed, exhausted and catching my breath. My body ached as I was carried back to my chair.

I'd discuss the next visit's goals with the JF specialists and then head back to Tyngsboro for a good night's sleep. Well, to be honest, I didn't have to wait that long. I could never stay awake on the ride home because I was so wiped out.

The payoff from my work at Journey Forward was everywhere in my life. The mental and physical benefits ranged from the pleasure of a good, intense workout to the sense that my life had purpose and meaning. This helped my attitude at school and at home.

Another big benefit was that I no longer needed the Hoyer lift. My increase in upper body strength meant I could graduate to a slide board. I still needed to be spotted while I made the transfer, but it was a huge improvement not to have to be slung into and out of bed.

Not that everything was perfect or that I was living in bliss. I wasn't looking for that. There were the usual serious daily challenges, and the long-term view of my life was a bummer sometimes. But I was focused on living day to day and becoming stronger. For my sanity I wanted to know that I was in motion, and I wanted to feel that my life had meaning. I wanted my paralysis to be a fact rather than an identity.

If it hurts a little, it's probably good for you. And the tattoo gun definitely hurts a little. But I want this. I've wanted it for some time now. I have something to say, and I want to say it forever.

The tattoo is just one word written across my bicep, but it sums up what's most important to me. Compared to that, a little discomfort is nothing. Actually, the pain makes the message feel even more real and true.

The holidays came and went. As usual, I spent Christmas Eve with Dad and Kim and their son Ryan, had Christmas at home with Mom and Sam, and visited my brother Ian and his family soon afterward. Ian and Angela had their son, Nicholas, just two days after I got my driver's license and eight months before I broke my neck. I was a seventeen-year-old uncle, but little Nick would learn to walk before I did. I had hoped that when I came back from Atlanta, as he was taking his first unassisted steps, I could join him and we'd play in the yard together, kicking a soccer ball and swinging a baseball bat. I wanted to build a bond with him as our bodies improved, and I wanted to share with him what I'd learned as a little athlete. Instead I watched him start to walk and then soon afterward begin to run.

Nick was a total wake-up call for me. When he was born I realized I was no longer the baby of the family. I had one of my first visions of myself as an adult, caring for a child the way I saw Ian caring for Nick. That father-son bond was amazing. I also felt motivated as Nick started running around, partly because I wanted to recover before Nick really understood why I wasn't out there with him and partly because I hoped someday to have what he and Ian had together. I wanted to be a dad, but I worried it would be hard to find someone interested in a guy in a chair. Most women probably thought I couldn't be a father or would be weirded out by thinking about it. I could explain it, but how would I ever get to that point in a conversation with someone?

Ian, Nick, and I were all starting from scratch, figuring it out as we went. It was all beautiful and strange and hard. It was family. It was life.

Other than Nicholas, maybe the best part of Christmas was knowing that Paul Sickinger and I had collected over three hundred winter coats for the homeless as part of a Service Learning Project in Ms. Craig's class. It was nice thinking that some people were a little bit warmer in the middle of a cold Boston winter.

Not long after school started was January 16, the first anniversary of my accident. I had been in school during the day and then headed to JF for my usual Thursday session. I hadn't talked about the anniversary all day but mentioned to one of the specialists that it had been a year. He looked at me and said, "You didn't want to take a day to yourself?"

"Why would I?" I replied. He thought for a second, shrugged, and gave me a look as if to say, "Fair enough." The days still move forward, and so do I. I didn't feel like I needed to set aside a whole day to reflect. I do that as I go and deal with things as they come up.

As they did one March morning in my first period class, Business Marketing, with Ms. Craig. She and I had an unspoken signal in case something was wrong and I needed to leave. We had only used it twice, both times for low blood pressure. Now I needed to use it again.

I was fine at the start of class, but after about twenty minutes I felt a small headache coming on. I rarely get headaches but when I do it's usually because of autonomic dysreflexia (AD), that mysterious syndrome in my disconnected nervous system. It wasn't bad, so I waited to see how it played out. This was, of course, my usual mistake of not speaking up when something is wrong, not asking for help, not wanting to cause a fuss. There was another part of me, too, that didn't want any Jack-centered drama to happen at school. It's that voice we all have that says, "Be normal in public!"

Another ten minutes went by and the headache ramped up quickly. It was throbbing, and with each throb I couldn't help but cringe. After another five minutes it had really escalated. Me being me, though, I thought to myself, *It will pass.* Five minutes later the pain was almost unbearable, and my eyes actually started pulsating. So much for being normal.

I looked at Ms. Craig and nodded toward the door, and she nodded back. I packed up, asked Justin to open the door, and left the room heading for the elevator just twenty feet away.

I swear that elevator is the slowest in the world and of course when it's idle it sits on the first floor. So I had to wait until it woke up and came up. At this point the pain was so bad that I wasn't even acknowledging people as they walked by. All I could do was keep hitting the stupid elevator button even though I heard the machinery working.

I quickly lost the ability to combat the pain. It had overwhelmed me. The elevator opened and I rolled in and pretty much punched the first-floor button with my fist. At least I hoped I hit the right button, because things were a little blurry. The AD was short-circuiting my senses.

Then Justin came flying around the corner. I don't know if he got permission from Ms. Craig or just left because he figured I was in trouble. I was really glad to see him because the way things were going, I wasn't even sure I could make it to the nurse's office. But of course as we descended I kept telling him I was fine, even though I was lost in a fog of pain.

After what felt like an hour-long descent, the doors opened, I rolled out, told Justin to go back to class, and blindly turned the corner. I couldn't see or hear and had to navigate the hallway by braille. I dragged my left hand along the trophy case lining the wall. At the end I made two quick left turns into the nurse's office.

It's a pretty small room, so I paused in the doorway to keep from running into something. I saw a blur, which I figured was Debbie in the back storage area. It wasn't unusual for me to show up in the doorway, so she didn't react at first. Well, not that I noticed. She could've asked me a question, but I wasn't able to hear or answer her.

I was trapped in the headache. All I could do was mutter, "Dysreflexic, dysreflexic," in between its pulses. I couldn't hear my own voice, so I had no idea if she was hearing me.

She was. Debbie quickly wrapped a blood pressure cuff around my arm and started to pump it up. My vision had improved a tiny bit, but every time my head throbbed, my eyes zoomed in. It's hard to explain, but it was like my vision was switching from blurry to clear and dark to light at the same time. I was submerged in the pain, but some little part of me was still able to think, *Hey, that's kind of cool.* I saw Debbie write down my blood pressure on a notepad, and it was about double my norm.

Sitting next to Debbie and suffering the unbearable headache took me back to the terrible times in Boston when the nurses changed my IV, waking me from the peace of a dead sleep into a world of pain. That's a place and time I never like to return to.

The spike in pain and blood pressure, not to mention possible dysreflexia complications, was too much for a school nurse to take on. Her job was to keep me stable until EMTs arrived. Debbie made the call, and guess who showed up? The same EMTs who had twice plopped me onto a stretcher a few months earlier. They probably see a lot of repeat customers, but I still had to wonder what they were thinking when they saw me again.

For my fellow students at Tyngsboro High, if you ever wondered why the school suddenly called a "No Pass Rule" that morning, now you know. You were stuck in your classrooms until the EMTs wheeled me out to the ambulance.

We raced to the hospital, the EMTs rushed me into the ER, and . . . I suddenly felt fine. Really, I did. I was 100 percent back to normal in a matter of minutes. The bizarreness of AD is that it can arrive mysteriously and disappear mysteriously. Some random fire alarm was pulled somewhere in the two-thirds of my body I no longer control and then just as randomly turned off. But because it's a fire alarm, we can never assume it's a false alarm.

Whenever this stuff happened it could be life-threatening, or it could be nothing. That's the body I live in.

I should have been happy that nothing serious was wrong, but you can imagine how irritated I was knowing I had caused a minor lockdown at my school all so that I could end up at a hospital for no good reason.

It was sometimes hard for me not to hold a grudge against

the weirdness of my injury. It was never a simple equation. If I'd lost a leg or an eye, the docs could have given me a prosthetic and I would have gone back out into life knowing what I had to work with. With the SCI, though, every time something crazy happened, my body felt like a stranger I would never truly understand. At times like this, when I was feeling a little sorry for myself, it seemed like anything that could go wrong did go wrong. From my bizarre response to a saline flush to a meaningless AD crisis in Business Marketing, if there was a 0.1 percent chance of something happening, it seemed to happen.

Oh well. I was over it, mostly. Life goes on, no matter how strange. Despite my misadventures in health care, the good news was that as the end of the school year approached, my classes continued to go well. It was definitely one of my best years for grades.

As the third trimester got underway, I could see the horizon rapidly approaching. High school was nearly over. All these kids I'd known and hung out with and become friends with in classes, hallways, and sports teams for the last twelve years would soon start to scatter.

I had to sort out this feeling that I was being left behind. I was a positive-thinking kid, but I was a realist too. There was a part of me that was afraid I wouldn't figure out what I should do with my life before it had passed me by. I knew my sense of being left behind was only as true as I let it be but knowing that didn't make it any less real.

How much of what I was feeling was the ordinary sadness of a high school senior acknowledging the end of childhood? How much of it was the fear that I was stuck driving my chair down the slow lane of life and still dependent on so many people?

And how much of it was the realization that the typical high points of senior year were likely to be a disappointment for a guy in a wheelchair? The end of senior year was supposed to be the most fun, a time where senior week and prom and graduation created indelible memories to share with each other for the rest of our adult lives.

This was kind of a complicated idea for me, though, because I was never the kind of guy who got too excited about formal events, like getting dressed up for a dance or putting on a robe to walk across a stage. On the other hand, I knew that because of the wheelchair, I might feel robbed of the experience. It sounds like a contradiction, I know, but I guess I wanted the most out of the time I had left with my high school friends, even if that meant dealing with going to prom in a chair.

It's almost expected that a book about a kid in high school is supposed to build up to some big climax around prom and graduation, but that's not my story. My book begins at its climax, the crisis of my adolescence—the failed frontside rodeo in Eric's yard—and then plays out the consequences to find what meaning there is to be found.

For me, the purpose and meaning of life has always been in the little things that you realize, or the goals you accomplish, or the experience you share with someone. For prom and senior week and graduation to become indelible memories I shared with friends forever, they would have to include those little things.

As it turned out, they mostly didn't. Most of the busy week (prom on a Friday, graduation the next Friday, with Senior Week in between) was a big fuss with lots of logistics and not many meaningful moments. But there were exceptions, like when I asked Devon to prom while we were riding the school elevator.

During third trimester, Devon always rode with me down to

the first floor after first period. So I planned ahead. After the door closed and the elevator began its creaky descent, I asked her to do me a favor and reach into my backpack, which was hooked onto the back of my chair, to pull out a folded piece of paper. She did, and then I asked her to open it. What she saw there was the word "Prom?" written in my shitty handwriting.

Devon looked at me and smiled. We'd become really close since the accident, and she had pretty much been waiting for me to ask. Looking back, I guess it was obvious that if I went to prom, I would go with Devon, but for a while I guess neither of us knew whether I wanted to go. And to be honest I stayed awake several nights thinking about it. I didn't want to go through the hassle of getting ready, taking pictures, and the whole ordeal that is prom night, especially since I couldn't dance. Prom is this weird symbol for entering adulthood, where you dress up in clothes no kid would ever wear and then dance like you're totally free.

So what would it mean to me?

But then I thought, *What if I don't go?* What else would I be doing? I thought about my friends going to prom without me and knew I would regret not going. Prom itself might not end up being memorable, but I knew I'd always remember the decision *not* to go.

Devon had been giving me time to figure it out. Now she gave me a hug, the doors opened, and we moved on to our next class. As much as I disliked that elevator, I was really happy it gave us that private moment together.

Prom was . . . okay. Devon and I went through the typical experience. She looked beautiful in a light-blue dress, and I wore a tie to match. We gathered outside the elementary school with our group of friends and their parents so we could all take pictures before we got into the limo. We were headed to a country club just over the border in New Hampshire, although I was so tuned out of the whole prom thing that I didn't even know our destination until Devon told me.

Justin had to carry me from the manual chair into the limo, and then back into the chair once we arrived. I was used to people seeing me so helpless, but I can't say I liked it. It kind of undermined the whole pretense of wearing a tux to look like an adult.

Once we reached the country club the group went down the stairs while Devon and I searched for the elevator. The club was a nice enough place. We ate some dinner and listened to whatever was on the radio. After the dinner, most of my friends went to dance while I hung out with Derek and Mike at the table. I didn't move much at all because the thick carpets made rolling around almost impossible. After a few hours we rounded up our group and went back to the afterparty at my place. I must have had twenty-five people packed into my apartment, and it was a blast. Everyone slept over: most were on the floor, some were in tents, and one even crashed in my van. It felt really good to have all of my friends together for a big night before we all graduated.

So prom wasn't much of a milestone, but it was a good time with my friends, and that's what mattered. I wouldn't have gained anything by not going. Even though I watched prom more than I participated, I was glad I went. "Live and learn" is a cliché, but the only way to learn from life is to get out there and live it. Try new things, go new places.

More than most kids my age, I knew there were no second chances in life, so why hold back?

Which meant I wasn't going to blow off the Senior Week excursions either. I was pretty sure the trips wouldn't be much better than prom, but so what?

I asked Eric Morrison if he wouldn't mind driving me to the activities. We'd been friends and competitors since the good old days of youth baseball, and now he was one of my closest friends, one member of the group who saw me, not the injury.

The week of trips was notable mostly because I got some experience of the world of accessibility problems. Of course I had dealt with access issues ever since my "recreational" excursions in Atlanta, but this was something different every day. On Monday we went on a yearbook signing boat cruise in Boston, which was fun other than the fact that I almost fell into the water while crossing a sketchy ramp getting off the boat. Tuesday I followed Eric and my friends around eighteen mini-golf holes, and while I couldn't play, we laughed a lot and it was weirdly maybe the most accessible trip of the week. Wednesday was a day at the beach, so that definitely wasn't going to work. Eric went and I stayed home. And Thursday was a hot ninety-five-degree day at Six Flags, where I basically drove my power chair from feature to feature and held my friends' stuff while they went on rides.

Friday wasn't a trip at all, just a cookout on the high school football field, and while access wasn't a problem it wasn't exactly a place I could forget my injury.

As a soon-to-be high school graduate, and someone who had learned a lot in the school of hard knocks, I felt like I was pretty ready to face the world. But after Senior Week it felt like maybe the world wasn't ready for me. I already knew plenty of local business owners who refused to spend a few thousand dollars to put in an automatic door. If this was the best time in history to be disabled, I hated to think what it had been like for the generations before me.

And then there's human behavior, the problem that a good ramp and an automatic door can't fix. I'm talking about people in public who make me feel small or invisible. The worst thing to say someone in a chair is nothing at all, but it happens all the time. Passersby look past me, like they want to get away from the kid in the wheelchair. And introducing myself to someone new can be really tough when they won't look at me. A lot of it has to do with not being at eye level. At times I end up talking to myself when someone stops paying attention.

All of which made it bittersweet when Ms. Craig gave me one of the business awards at graduation. (And Devon won the other award, which was cool.) Ms. Craig knew that while I wasn't an academic star, I worked hard because of who she was and how she treated me. Ms. Craig was the ideal adult for someone like me to encounter in public, and I was going to miss having her in my life every day.

Graduation was another milestone that felt more like a fork in the road. One hundred and seventeen graduates, plus hundreds of family and friends, sat in an unair-conditioned gymnasium on a hot June day. The students were on chairs in the middle while everyone else filled up the bleachers, all of us listening to the principal and valedictorian talk to us about believing in our futures. Students were arranged by height, which meant that because I was perched up on my power chair, I sat in the back and would be the last to receive my diploma. The amplified drone of the voices merged with the sounds of the restless audience and the ceiling fans.

Sometime during the speeches I figured it out. The school hadn't set up the usual stage this year. Why? Because of me and my chair, I'm sure, though no one ever said a word to me about it. Tyngsboro High always did right by me. I was impressed, if a little embarrassed.

Graduation was a day that I knew was coming for so long, but as I sat there it didn't feel like a phase of life was over. It was hard to imagine that starting the next day I probably wouldn't see 80 percent of the other graduates at all. I spent twelve years of school with basically the same 120ish kids and then—Poof!—we went our separate ways.

It definitely makes you think, which is what I was doing during the ceremony. *What will I do for work? Am I going to live in my mom's house forever?* I had plans to go to UMass-Lowell in September, but I didn't have many other options. It was too soon to live on my own, so I had to commute from home. If the accident hadn't happened, I might have shopped around to try to play football at a regional D3 school, but that was a world I had left far behind.

When my time finally came, I rolled up to the front, got my business award and my diploma, smiled, heard some cheers, and rolled back into my place. That was it. A few minutes later we shuffled out the doors to the lit football field where we hung out and took pictures until the crowd dispersed and our lives changed.

Years from now, would I look back on these moments and fantasize about going back to high school? Or would I be happy enough and busy enough in life that looking backward seemed unnecessary?

Time to find out, I guess.

Summer was here. I was a quadriplegic eighteen-year-old with childhood officially behind me. Not looking backward meant I had to lean forward into adulthood. The fact that I was leaning in from a wheelchair while living in my mom's house was frustrating but not impossible. I had to deal with it, embrace it if possible, and move on. I wasn't living the dream, but I wasn't dreaming to live either.

One of the first things I did was get a tattoo, a big cursive *Family* written across my left bicep. Sure, being stuck at home was hard, but nothing was more important to me than the people who had given me so much unconditional love and support. I'd been thinking about the tattoo for a few months. Family was the rock I anchored myself to when my life was turned upside down. They'd meant everything to me that past year. I was so proud of Mom and Dad and Sam, and so thankful they'd been there for me through the worst times. I wanted to symbolize that permanently.

The next thing I did was go for a driving evaluation. I'd put it off for months because I was sure it would be a hassle and just another reminder of how I wasn't capable of getting back behind the wheel. I wondered if I'd ever be able to drive. I really missed the freedom of the pre-injury days when I could jump into the old Explorer and visit friends or cruise to Nashoba. Anyway, I showed up thinking I could only get assessed for the possibility of driving someday, but I ended up getting in the van with the instructor and driving around a practice course behind the building. Within five minutes I knew that I was going to be able to do it. I was ecstatic. Part of my future that had seemed dark to me suddenly opened up and became bright again.

Chalk up another victory for the core strengthening workouts at Journey Forward.

In the meantime, I occasionally hit the open road in my power chair. The farthest I went was to a party at Paul's, a couple miles away. He lived near Flint's Corner, which meant I had to drive up Old Stonehill Road past The Wasteland and Eric Vadenais's place. It seems hard to believe, but this was the first time in the year and a half since the accident I had been back to that spot.

I thought about simply powering uphill past Eric's to show

I didn't care, but I wanted to stop and face it. All I could do was stare at the yard and that little shed at the top where I launched. There were other houses around me, and some cars coming and going, but I didn't notice them. It was just me and that little hill.

Really, it was tiny. And yet it totally changed my life.

Like I keep saying: it's the little things that make the biggest difference.

At the time, though, I was thinking something else. I had been through hell but had found little bits of heaven along the way. I was a survivor. So maybe it was a bit dramatic, but one line rose up to the surface of my brain: I'm back, motherfucker. I felt a little surge of something. If it wasn't invincibility, it was certainly pride and resilience.

Then I turned away and continued up and around the corner to the party at Paul's.

14

WHAT'S NEXT?

What does resilience look like? Sometimes I'm alone and worried that the challenges are too big, but over the last two years I've learned that if I keep pushing, I'll get through it. If I take life day by day, I'll survive and sometimes even thrive.

When I look in the mirror, I only have to remind myself what I've been through. That's enough to keep me going. And so that's what resilience looks like. Me, in the mirror.

My motto became two simple words and a question mark. When I reached a goal, or even when I felt like I was stuck in a rut, I looked around and asked, "What's next?"

That's how I got rid of the slide board. It had been a huge improvement over the Hoyer lift, but it was still one of those annoyances of quadriplegic life. My upper body was finally strong enough to make the big leap rather than several little ones to cross the board, so I said to my mom, "I'm not using it anymore." I just dug one hand into the cushion of the chair and one into the bed and pushed myself over as hard as I could. From then on it only got easier.

I kept asking myself what else I could be doing to get better. There were days when I found it hard to focus on the next step, but I knew the only way to reach the ultimate goal—to get out of the chair and walk—was to keep inching forward. I set realistic, manageable goals to take me in the right direction.

My hard work paid off when I was recognized by the High Fives Foundation. High Fives is a nonprofit started by Roy Tuscany, a promising competitive skier who, in 2006, suffered an SCI while landing from a hundred-foot jump. After a few years of intense therapy, Roy regained enough movement to get back on the slopes. But he didn't forget what he'd gone through. He created High Fives to give other people the kind of support he'd received during his recovery.

I had been in touch with High Fives for a year and had applied for support. Right before graduation I finally heard that I was a High Fives Athlete and was awarded the $10,000 grant we had asked for! It would fund an extra day per week at Journey Forward for an entire year. In their recognition, High Fives specifically talked about how hard I was working to improve, so I guess they saw me as a safe investment.

High Fives set up an athlete page for me on their site and asked for an inspiring quote. I chose something Herb Brooks, the coach of the "Miracle on Ice" 1980 Olympic US Hockey Team, said to his guys: "Be uncommon. A group of common men go nowhere." I didn't think I was uncommon, but I figured it was something to aspire to.

With the grant and the funds raised by the Jack Trottier Open Golf Tournament in September, I had another year of Journey Forward to be excited about, especially since I'd be working out three days a week instead of two.

I was still waiting on my severed nerves to reconnect and talk to my brain, but I knew my body would be ready when they did. Part of my motivation was the fact that I'd seen too many people stop trying. They thought that after a few months or even a few years of not seeing any return of neuro function, they should give up hope. But I couldn't begin to understand that. I couldn't imagine accepting that I would be in the chair for the rest of my life. I knew there wasn't a cure yet, and that there may not be one for quite some time, but until then I was going to keep working. What else could I do?

At the very beginning of my journey, when I lay there in the snow waiting to get up, I had no idea what kind of Herculean effort would be required. As I lay in the hospital beds in Boston and Atlanta, waiting to stand up and walk out of the hospital, I still had no idea.

Eventually I stopped waiting for a spontaneous, miraculous recovery, but that didn't mean that I had given up on miracles. I just knew that the path to a miracle, should it happen, was going to be built with hard work and determination. I couldn't lie down and wait for recovery. I would stand up and walk toward my future, assisted as necessary until I no longer needed the assistance.

I had learned the hard way that the biggest hurdles in life require more mental toughness than physical ability. As long as I remembered that, I was winning the battle. Or at least I was still in the fight.

I had to admit, though, that mental toughness didn't come naturally to me. Sure, as a kid I could take a hit in football or obsess over a lacrosse technique for hours, but that's because all through childhood that stuff came easily to me. Working hard at sports felt good because I succeeded and was noticed for it. All those "tough" things I accomplished in sports weren't actually huge challenges for me.

Honestly, I wasn't the hardest worker. Not that I like to admit it, and not that I didn't try, but I rarely stuck with a challenge if the rewards weren't immediate. Other than sports, I never found something that I wanted to diligently pursue. I didn't join clubs, and I didn't have hobbies. If I picked up an instrument, I'd learn half a song and then put it in a corner to collect dust. (I blame Sam for this, actually, since she inherited all the musical talent in my family.)

At the time of the accident, I was a typical high school quarterback. That isn't necessarily a bad thing, but it isn't a great thing, either. I was naturally athletic, reasonably smart, and pretty popular. I had enough confidence to get me through the day. Life was very good. I worked out because I enjoyed staying fit. I tried new sports because they seemed fun. But being a good athlete isn't the same as being tough.

After the accident, everything was different. The challenge was constant, and the road ahead was always uphill. Nothing came easily. I worked out because otherwise I'd deteriorate. Exercise was no longer about having fun—although that still happened—it was about gaining independence. Working out and training for recovery became a crucial part of maintaining myself both physically and mentally.

I couldn't give up on recovery the way I gave up on guitar. I didn't have a choice. My new body required a new work ethic. To give up was bad for my health and bad for my future. Not that there weren't times when I felt like quitting. Luckily, these were fleeting moments or dark late-night hours that could be driven away with a little sunshine.

I had learned, deep down, that I could not quit no matter how hard things were. That's mental toughness, I think, and it became as much a part of me as my unresponsive legs.

I didn't learn it on my own, though. I had a lot of help along the way, especially from my parents. The fact that Mom never left my side for months was the greatest possible lesson in resilience and persistence. Day and night, month after month, and now year after year, I have watched her give everything, sacrifice anything—sleep, money, time—to look after me. I don't think there is anything tougher than a mother's love.

And without Dad's coaching I would never have toughened up. He let me know early on that life wasn't a game anymore, that shit had gotten real. Throughout my time in Atlanta I was still in the "I'll be better in a few months" phase, but again and again he had to shake his head and straighten me out.

After I came home, Dad talked to me on the back deck about how I'd better be clear-eyed enough to really understand how hard this was going to be. About the discipline I'd need to stay in the fight. As hard as it could be to hear it from Dad, what I liked was that it was a continuation of the kind of advice he gave me all through childhood. If I wanted to try something, he made sure I was committed. If it was a new sport, I had to play it through to the end of the season. "Never leave teammates high and dry, Jack," he said.

Likewise, Kim was a great role model and advocate for me. She was a big part of the success of the golf tourney, but more importantly she went to battle with the insurance companies again and again on my behalf. Insurance in Massachusetts is a pain in the ass in terms of what they cover and don't cover, and each year they screw up something. Kim is my go-to for that fight. She'll hop on the phone for two hours to set them straight. Plus, on a personal level, she's always been someone I could turn to when I was trying to solve a problem.

I owed a lot to all my trainers too. It sounds corny, but they all brought something different and meaningful into my life. Each trainer and each facility had their own approach and their own philosophy when it came to disability and wellness. Patty and Cathi in Atlanta helped me to believe that I could live a more independent life. The trainers at Journey Forward increased the scope of that independence. Together they gave me the right combination of hope and honesty I needed to hear, and the skills I needed to go forward. From all of them I learned that while my new life wouldn't be easy, it could be as full and real as any able-bodied life. Other SCI patients had survived and thrived before me, so I could too.

I had my family, my trainers, my friends. I could deal with the occasional flare-up of anxiety. I also had a referral to see a psychologist, but I never made an appointment. I didn't reject professional help, really, but I didn't seek it out. I didn't feel the need. I guess it's not surprising for a guy who despite being blind and deaf from a sudden AD headache tells his friend to go back to class because he's "fine," but it's just who I am. I pretty much need a full-on disaster before I ask for help. That's who I was when I lay paralyzed in the snow for ten minutes, and it's who I was a year and a half later.

I respect anyone who decides to talk with a professional about how they're coping with a crisis, but I decided—despite all my crazy anxious nights—to figure things out on my own. I dealt with my stress by reading books and watching psychology and philosophy videos that had a positive influence on me. They weren't catered to me personally like a conversation with a therapist, but they taught me a lot about myself, and I was able to use that to keep my head straight. Anything that helped me make order out of chaos got my full attention. It wasn't so much that I found thinkers who I could follow—that was never my style—but that I was searching for the bits and pieces of common sense and wisdom that I could use to make sense of the life I was living.

People think of problems as locks, answers as keys. And sometimes that's true, but I've found that answers are usually like a compass that helps you change direction a little. Or even a lot. Making that change might take a while, but you keep thinking about it until you do. It's not like someone can say, "Hey, you need mental toughness!" and you say, "Okay!" and then radically change your life. You have to work at it, think about it, learn it for yourself.

═══════════════

Wind blowing cold and hard in my face, my body shaking, my arms strained to the point of breaking: I've never felt better in my life. Before me, the Mad River Valley and the Green Mountains of Vermont are spread out like a painting. And I'm in the painting! I'm a colored dot cruising down one of the wide white slopes of Sugarbush.

This is not a dream.

I once lived in a daily relationship with speed, g-force, balance, strength, and risk, but I haven't felt it since the accident. Now here I am, back on the snow, alive and flying.

Another part of mental toughness is not being afraid to try new things. This was always a problem for me outside of sports. I didn't want to fail. I nervously weighed the pros and cons before making decisions based on whether or not I thought I could be good at it, or at least that it would be good for me.

The accident and its aftermath taught me to come to grips with the fact that the only way to learn anything is to make mistakes. The first big lessons came from the recreational therapy trips in Atlanta. There were a thousand reasons why I didn't want to do those, but I came out of it a little older and wiser. Flash forward several months and there I was power chairing down the back roads of Tyngsboro! Lesson learned, I think, although I still found myself wrestling with the fear of making a fool of myself sometimes.

How do we learn how bad an idea is if we don't try? My friends and I often tell stories about crazy things we did and at the end we inevitably ask, "Why the hell did we do that?" But I know I'd rather shake my head and ask that question than sit there without stories to tell and say, "I wish I'd tried it."

When winter came, I had a big decision to make. High Fives was connected with Vermont Adaptive, which offers adaptive ski lessons at Sugarbush Ski Resort in Warren, Vermont, and they had provided funds for me to take part. They covered expenses for my tickets, trainers, and lodging. It would be my first time back on snow since the accident. I was super excited about returning to the slopes, but I also had second thoughts. Would it be too difficult? Too cold? Was I strong enough? Would I fail and be disappointed in myself?

I had been named a High Fives Athlete, so I figured I should own the title and get back to doing athlete things. I said yes and started getting ready. Over the next few weeks I dug up all the snow gear—helmet, goggles, gloves, etc.—that had been buried over the previous two years. I bought a new jacket and snow pants online, since my old ones had been cut off by the EMTs. I laid out all of it on a therapy mat on my floor and made sure everything was ready to go.

I also spent a lot of time online looking up images and instructions for the sit-ski contraption I'd use at Sugarbush. My version was a bi-ski, which was pretty much two three-sided boxes—one to sit in and the other for my feet—bolted to a pair of skis. A paraplegic generally uses a mono-ski because they have better upper body strength to balance with. Even with two skis, though, I wondered how I was going to stay up without total control of my core muscles, or how I would lean into my poles on turns without full triceps. I had recovered a lot of function, but I wasn't sure it was enough.

Either way, as late February 2015 arrived, it was time to find out. Dad and I were booked for a three-day stay at the Sugar Lodge, only half a mile from the mountain. With our usual navigation problems, we managed to turn a three-hour drive into a four-hour trip because we took the wrong exit. That was all forgotten as we approached the hotel. Over the treetops we could see the top of 4,083-foot Mt. Ellen, the tallest of Sugarbush's six peaks.

I hadn't seen such a big ski mountain since our trip to Colorado. Most of my time on snow was at little Nashoba with its 240-foot vertical drop. Sugarbush, with a 2,600-foot vertical, was almost eleven times higher. Seeing that peak over the trees really got my attention. I was excited but at the same time couldn't help but wonder what the hell I had gotten myself into. This was also the first time since Atlanta I had stayed overnight anywhere other than home or a hospital.

I wasn't surprised to find some accessibility problems in Warren, Vermont. I just didn't expect it to be as bad as it was. Central

Vermont in the middle of winter isn't ideal when it comes to wheelchair maneuverability, but there are some pretty simple rules for making public places accessible. The Sugar Lodge was following those rules, more or less, but they weren't making it easy. The parking lot was uneven and icy, and the wheelchair ramp was blocked by ice and soft snow. I plowed through for a ways but got stuck until Dad gave me a solid push.

Other people might have complained to the hotel staff to get the ramp cleared, but my dad and I are both the type of people who say, "Screw it," and do it ourselves.

At least the lodge had an accessible bathroom. It wouldn't have been an option otherwise. If you have an SCI, you might be on a schedule for bathroom breaks. For me, it's generally every four hours. I can wait up to seven hours if I have to, but it's not a great idea because I'd risk an AD episode. Traveling away from home like this meant always having a plan for those four-hour intervals. I was already thinking about tomorrow and hoping I'd have enough time on the slopes before I needed that next break.

We settled into our small room, where Dad had to push the twin beds farther apart to make room for my chair, but then we had to go out again for dinner before the restaurants closed. We found a pub called The Elusive Moose, but their wheelchair ramp was blocked by a snowdrift. We got back in the van and headed to the only other option, The Big Picture Theater & Café—a little 1950s-style cinema that only showed one movie at a time. It was eight p.m., and we were the only customers. The menu had about ten items, but we were excited to have found something to eat before it was too late.

Dad and I joked about the evening so far, but really I think we just had the wrong expectations. We figured a big mountain like

Sugarbush would have a bustling town with lots of options for fast food and hotels, but Warren only had about 1,700 residents. I thought of Tyngsboro with its 11,500 people as a small town, but it seemed like a metropolis to me while we sat there alone eating our sandwiches.

So the trip was already a wake-up call, and that was a good thing. I had to be strategic to get around in my chair, and I had to be adaptable rather than cautious and conservative about what to do and where to go. During the long months stuck at home, I had longed for the unexpected, and here it was. I knew I could figure things out; I always did. I was having an adventure already, even if the first mountain I conquered was only four inches of slush.

The next stage of my hero's journey was to get a night's sleep. I had made it up the lodge's ramp in one try, probably because the temperature was around zero and the slush had turned to ice. Now I was stuck in a small twin bed with pillows propped around me and between my legs. (At home I had a special air mattress with softball-size pockets that I could blow up to take pressure off different parts of my body.) I might have accepted a pile of rocks to sleep on in exchange for a quiet room. It's comical the way my dad snores. It's all night long, and it's inhumanly loud, like someone sawing wood next to a microphone. Worse, he falls asleep as soon as his head hits the pillow, leaving everyone else within fifty feet to suffer. He and I hadn't gone on a trip together for a long time, and now I remembered why.

I couldn't help but laugh as I lay there facing the wall and imagining the next day. I kept thinking, *I'm really here. I'm really doing this thing.* I pictured myself in the sit-ski and imagined replicating the motions I learned from YouTube. I was curious if my hands and arms could endure the entire day, if I could hold the poles for steering without being able to clench my fists, if I could even put ski gloves on. I was anxious to try.

I needed to fall asleep.

Dad's alarm went off at six a.m. for some reason. We only had to drive half a mile for a nine-thirty appointment with Vermont Adaptive. If it was up to me, I would have set the alarm for nine, but Dad is an early bird and a big believer in planning ahead. I hadn't seen six a.m. in months, and the morning light seemed weird. I had my eyes half closed as we worked together on my stretching and getting me warmed up for the day. At home if I woke up cold, I'd sit under a heat fan in my bathroom, but that wasn't an option here.

Before the accident when I hit the mountain, I rarely wore anything warmer than a T-shirt under my jacket and some thin long underwear under my snow pants. Those days were gone, and I knew that riding the sit-ski wouldn't get my blood pumping the way able-bodied skiing did. So it was all about the layers. For my lower body, Dad put on my new thermal long johns, new black insulated snow pants, and thick ski socks. He fastened the nylon binder around my torso and covered it with a thermal top layer and a crew neck sweatshirt the Lowell Fire Department gave me and Paul in honor of our project collecting coats for the homeless.

Breakfast was upstairs, but of course there was no elevator. Dad fetched it for both of us, we ate quickly, I hit the bathroom, and then I was ready to go. I had a mountain to conquer, and I already felt amped up and trapped in that small room. I finished dressing by throwing on my yellow High Fives beanie and my new ski jacket. The crazy thing about the jacket is that it also had a High Fives emblem on it, even though I bought it randomly online. When it arrived I thought, *What are the odds?* and decided it was destiny.

To reach my destiny, I first had to conquer the walkway outside, where I got stuck again. It took some pulling and pushing from my dad to get through. The whole isn't-it-funny-our-lodge-doesn't-give-a-shit-about-wheelchairs thing was getting old fast. But Mt. Ellen was up there waiting for me, and the sky was crystal clear.

A few minutes later we passed the huge, empty parking lots—empty because it was a weekday morning between school vacation and college spring break—and pulled up to the main lodge. There were a few handicap parking spaces and a door at ground level. So far so good. As I exited the van I felt a familiar wave of cold air and excitement wash over me. I heard the sound of a high-speed quad chairlift as it turned the corner to scoop up skiers on its way back up the mountain, and it reminded me of my childhood at Nashoba from the early years all the way up to becoming a snowboard instructor. I had forgotten how much a ski mountain feels like a second home to me. I hadn't realized how much I missed it.

Of course before the accident, I never would have noticed that there was a short, steep, icy wheelchair-unfriendly slope to descend toward the lodge door. I thought to myself, *Really? I have to work for this? To have fun I need get through all this bullshit first?* My dad and I just looked at each other and laughed. It was definitely more of a "Are you kidding me?" laugh than a "That's funny!" laugh.

Dad spotted me while I went down the slope backward, blindly and slowly, with the front wheels spinning uselessly up in the air, until finally I rolled through the door into a classic ski lodge, a big open room with a fireplace and walls lined with cubbies from floor to ceiling.

We found the Vermont Adaptive office just past the fireplace.

Suddenly I felt nervous, which was unusual. I was cool, calm, and collected when I played in a state semi-final varsity football game, and when I competed in big air and slopestyle snowboard competitions at Nashoba, but this was different. I guess the difference was that the big games and competitions were merely challenges. This felt more like a life-changing event. Something I had figured was impossible was right in front of me. I was about to get back on snow!

The problem with being nervous was that it made me lightheaded. This was a relatively new phenomenon, and it was annoying. Just when I was fighting a stomach full of butterflies, I also had to keep from passing out. I could only hope that when we got out of the overheated lodge into the cold air I'd wake up. The last thing I wanted was to pass out mid-run and slam into a tree. I was especially worried because traveling downward on a slope wasn't the best position to keep my blood flowing. When I need to increase my blood flow, I lean back. Leaning forward down the mountain would have the opposite effect.

Meeting my lead instructor, Gildon, gave me confidence. He'd moved to the US from Israel years ago, and I could tell from his worn-out gear—helmet, snow pants, and jacket all patched with duct tape—that he was both a serious skier and an experienced one.

I knew from my research that I wouldn't be skiing independently. As a quadriplegic, I couldn't develop total control over the process. Gildon would be tethered to my sled and controlling my descent. But the sooner I learned to turn and control my speed, the less he would have to do.

I finally got to look at the sled up close. The back was low, so I worried I might not be able to hold myself upright. The cushion in the box was thin, which meant I might get sore before too long. But I had to let the worries go. The sit-ski was sleek and blue and all mine for the next three days.

Dad picked me up and placed me gently into the sled.

I had to figure out what to do with my hands. Dad and I had purchased oversized mittens before the trip, big enough that his hand could fit inside with mine. That way he could help get my thumb into the thumb hole. Then he held the outside of each mitten to keep my fingers from curling into a fist and wrapped them around the handles of the "riggers," short ski poles that have small skis at the bottom. Once my hands were attached to the handles and the forearm cuff was fastened, I still needed something to keep my hands from falling off the poles when skiing hard down the mountain. We were thinking they must have some kind of technical strap, but when we asked Gildon, he just looked at us and said, "Duct tape."

Perfect. They don't have time for fancy nonsense in Vermont. I was still feeling lightheaded, but I was locked in and taped down. It was time to hit the slopes. Dad put on my final fashion accessories—neck warmer, Oakley goggles, Bern helmet with my old GoPro camera and a new High Fives sticker that read #HelmetsAreCool—and I have to say that at least it looked like I knew what I was doing.

The helmet was the smartest thing I was wearing. Even though mine hadn't helped with my straight drop onto my neck, they really do work for most collisions. When you're a confident kid you don't think too much about them, but as I got older I saw how important they were. And then when I arrived in Atlanta and saw all the traumatic brain injury victims struggling in the gym or moving quietly through their darkened hallway, it got real for me. So many of those kids could have walked away from their accidents if they had worn a helmet.

At this point, Dad had stepped back to let the instructors do their thing. He didn't ask a lot of questions. He was more interested in how I felt physically and mentally. From the day of the accident Dad had worked hard to make life a little easier for me, to find solutions to problems. So he did a final check-in—"How are your hands, Jack? Do you feel alright in the seat?"—and then let Gildon do his job.

Gildon had worked with the Vermont Adaptive program for many years and only needed a few minutes to give me the basics: lean into my turns, put the rigger down as I leaned, use the edge of the skis to carve, and turn slightly uphill to slow down. This was all the same stuff I taught new riders when I was an instructor at Nashoba.

Before we left the office, Gildon grabbed the back of the sled and had me lean into a few imagined turns. And that's really all I needed. The rest of it would be finding my balance and applying my experience to a different kind of skiing.

Time to go. I pulled the goggles over my eyes. The only exposed skin was my nose. I went through a few turns in my head while Gildon and three other instructors suited up. A minute later they pushed me across the carpet and out the double doors into the snow.

Jogging quickly, they took me down a short ramp and then up to where they kept their skis. I didn't need the riggers until we started our run, so I had my hands on my lap and the riggers crossed over my legs.

Those few seconds zipping down the ramp threw me for a loop. It wasn't actually fast, but the fastest I'd moved in two years was when I cruised Tyngsboro at seven miles per hour in my power chair. I couldn't believe that I'd actually forgotten what speed felt like. I looked up at the mountain and felt a bit overwhelmed.

Well, I was sure we'd take it step by step before things got serious.

Or not. Once Gildon and crew clicked their boots into their skis, they pushed me straight to the chairlift, only a few hundred feet away. *Wait, what?* I turned my head to look up at Gildon, who was pushing the handle on the back of the sled.

I asked, "That's it? We're going right to the chairlift?"

"No worries, Jack. You'll be fine."

Did I trust him? Not really. I wasn't sure if he realized that my core and triceps would give out much more quickly than someone with full upper-body function.

Whatever. He was the expert, and I was here to go where the new Jack had never gone before. It was time to stop worrying and remember my motto: What's next?

I didn't say another word.

After a moment I felt a bit like the old Jack, actually, going for broke—not literally, I hoped—in a sport I'd never tried before. *Hell yeah*, I thought. *Let's go!* They couldn't see the smile on my face, but it was there.

We traveled through a vacant line to the Green Mountain Express Quad, and as we reached the operator, Gildon shouted over the engine of the chairlift, "Take it at full speed!"

Wait, what? Damn, Gildon was doing it to me again. For those who haven't gone skiing or snowboarding, newer riders and younger kids usually get on the lift at half the normal speed. I was trapped in this tiny contraption and he wanted me to hit the lift at full speed?

I couldn't believe what I was hearing, but I didn't care anymore. It might be fine, or it might be a train wreck. If he'd asked me what I thought, I would have simply said, "I'm in." I didn't want to back down, regardless of the risk. Obviously that kind of attitude hasn't always worked out for me, but the bitter moments have made the sweet ones all the sweeter.

And this was a sweet moment.

I kept my mouth shut and literally went along for the ride. As we slid quickly into place for the next quad chair, Gildon and another instructor stood on either side of me and bent to grasp the frame of the sled. With a "One . . . two . . . three" they lifted me up and slid the box over the seat while the skis fit firmly underneath.

Not bad. Trusting Gildon was paying off. They shifted me to the center of the seat, brought the safety bar down, and safety-clipped the sled to the back of the chairlift. Dad and the other instructors piled into the next quad chair behind us.

Not so bad, I repeated to myself as the lift accelerated and we climbed up three stories into the clear, cold, fresh mountain air. Suddenly another wave of memories and déjà vu swept over me. We didn't have big fast quad lifts at Nashoba, but the sensation was the same. Up in the air, I felt like I hadn't missed a day on the slopes, like the past two years hadn't been long enough or strange enough or difficult enough to make me forget what it felt like to be alive on the mountain.

I was right where I belonged.

We came up over the first peak, a few thousand feet in elevation, where another chair took skiers to the summit. Not me, though. At least Gildon wasn't going that far. It was a good call, since I'd already noticed a big drop in temperature from the base of the mountain.

I knew now that the instructors had things under control, but I was still skeptical about getting *off* the lift at full speed. Yet that's what we did. Just as the chair was slowed by the brakes on the lift, Gildon and his buddy lifted the back end of the sled, pushed me forward, kept me balanced, and steered me away from the lift to the top of the first trail. The name of the trail was, appropriately enough, Which Way. A choice and a challenge.

Gildon attached two permanent riggers (as opposed to the ones strapped to my hands) to the sides of the sit-ski. They sat high, not touching the snow, because they were only meant to stop the sled from tipping over if I wasn't able to do it myself. It's something Vermont Adaptive used for beginners like me. I thought of them as training wheels or bumpers in a bowling alley.

And just like that I was poised at the top of a ski trail for the first time in two years. The snow-covered Green Mountains stretched off into the distance, and the Mad River Valley lay below us like a pretty postcard. Little Warren was just an island of buildings in an ocean of trees.

Dad asked me how my hands felt, which wasn't a bad question considering they were trapped in mittens and wrapped in duct tape. I had no movement in my fingers, yet I was about to rely on them to help me descend a mountain?

I told him they were perfect.

"Ready?" asked Gildon.

"Ready."

Off we went, Gildon behind me holding onto my sled while I placed the riggers in the snow to practice my balance. Which Way was a blue square—an intermediate slope, not for beginners—and the first part was too steep and narrow to turn. Gildon maintained control until we made it to the wider trail, then it was my turn.

Gildon shouted over the noise of the wind that I should carve back and forth across the entire trail. That way I could keep a steady speed but still ski quickly enough to stay upright.

I couldn't really hear him at first, so I just did my own thing and stayed focused on not crashing. Luckily that worked pretty well. Within thirty seconds or so, my instincts took over and I began shifting my weight to carve like I used to on a snowboard. Gildon let go of the back of my sled and fell behind, connected now only by a tether tied to the sled. He limited my speed while I practiced my turns, using the riggers and leaning to each side.

It felt natural. I had pretty much figured out the idea of riding the sit-ski through careful study of videos, but on the slope all my years of snowboarding were kicking in. I flowed in and out of each turn nice and easy. Gildon had to keep my speed down, but other than that I was navigating on my own.

It felt absolutely amazing. I was high up on the slopes of a big ski mountain looking out over the beautiful world, and what I loved especially was that I was steering. I was traveling fast, I was traveling gracefully, and I was driving. It was liberating, to say the least. With the wide-open white slope ahead of me, I was free to choose where I wanted to go and how I wanted to get there. After the last two years of confinement, there was no better feeling in the world.

Speed and control. It was the first time in what felt like forever that I didn't have something in my way stopping me or slowing me down. I felt like I was leaving behind all the quadriplegic crap I go through every day. This was freedom instead of limitation, adventure instead of routine, risk instead of safety. All the little things that made me feel small had been left on the bottom of the mountain.

It had been years and years since I had taken a long run down a big mountain. I'd spent so much time in the Nashoba terrain park and on Nashoba's short trails, that I'd forgotten the exhilaration of a long, flowing trip downhill in a dance with gravity and time. All you hear is the sound of the skis as they carve though the snow. Your body is in tune with the mountain as you traverse the slope, feeling every little bump in the snow. Skiing is an art form. It really is.

As I swept through one high-speed turn after another, I felt the g-force, I felt the wind in my face, and I felt fully alive. I felt joy. I could not express any of it in words.

Free. So free. Descending the mountain while enjoying the view of the Vermont wilderness stretching out for many miles was something I will never forget.

Better yet, I was getting better quickly. We stopped a couple times during the run to catch our breath, and each time we took off again I felt a little more at home. Dad said, "Looks great, Jack!" and the instructors agreed.

We finished the first run and got right back on the lift. Before the second run we decided to take the safety riggers off and count on my arm strength to keep me from falling over.

I had a shaky start, falling only a few seconds into the run. It was a small fall—sliding only a few feet to a stop—and I didn't care one bit. I could have gone thirty miles an hour straight into the woods and I still would've been ecstatic. And just like when I flipped backward in my van with Luke, falling actually felt pretty good. I had to be careful to tuck in my arms so they weren't yanked backward, but I loved making contact with the snow. It was real. The more I can feel my body moving in space and interacting with the hard world the happier I am. Skidding across rough terrain and slowly coming to a stop is part of the dance with the mountain.

Each turn got more fluid, and I was slowly able to sweep wide back and forth across the trail to regulate my speed. That meant Gildon could ease up on the tether and let me take control. He only needed to step in when it was time to slow down and stop.

Every moment was extraordinary, but exhausting too. By the end of the second run I wasn't even sure if my arms were still attached to my body. My muscles burned like I'd just done a hard-core arm workout at Journey Forward, but I didn't say a word. I wanted more.

We went back up to the top for a third run. But by the end of that run my core temperature was dropping, and I had to look down to make sure my arms were still attached. I was literally dragging them across the snow because I couldn't pick them up. I figured it was a good time to end the session.

Part of me wanted to keep going all day, but I wasn't disappointed. Really, adaptive skiing was so much more amazing than I had dreamed it might be. All my doubts and fears had disappeared the moment I started downhill. It's like I discovered my old self and something new at the same time. To say I was happy was an understatement. I was thrilled.

I did it all again for the next two days. Uphill and downhill, uphill and downhill, pushing hard and finding my groove. Each run was a little better, each turn was a little sweeter. I guess I exceeded Gildon's expectations, since he gave me a hug and told me that he had never seen anyone progress as quickly as I did.

I have to confess that his comment moved me. The best thing about the trip was regaining the grace and freedom I hadn't felt in two years. And I was excited about how quickly I'd picked it up. But to hear from Gildon that I had surpassed his previous clients really fed my competitive spirit. I take things like that to heart.

So there I was, still in the race, even if the race was against myself and against the fear of defeat I'd carried with me since the accident. I'd stretched myself, challenged my limits, and pushed my body until I felt like dropping. If I was Sisyphus, I had carried a big chunk of the rock with me in the chairlift and left it on the mountain. If I was Alice, I'd come out of the rabbit hole perhaps a little stronger and a little wiser.

And I loved every second of it.

Life was not the same—not even close—but it was mine to live.

In the final two days, I took a few more falls, but nothing too serious, mostly just skidding out while trying to stop. Every rough contact with the snow shook me awake and made me feel even more alive.

After one fall, I waved off Dad and Gildon and the guys and said I just needed a minute. I lay there looking up at the blue sky and feeling the cold snow beneath me. There was adrenaline and exhaustion flowing through my veins and a sense of peace flooding my mind. Part of me wanted to ski forever, and the rest of me wanted to lay my head down on the snow and sleep. There were no snowflakes drifting down, no Jack drifting off into unconsciousness as an ambulance wailed in the distance. Instead, the sky was crystal clear, and I was simply happy to be where I was.

Ever since the accident I had kind of thought of myself as still in midair, figuring out what would happen to me. But in reality, I had fallen.

Yes, I had fallen. But I got up. That's what I do.

EPILOGUE

OCTOBER 20, 2019

It's been nearly seven years since my accident, and as I lay here thinking about what it means to live after you've blown apart the sixth vertebrae below your skull, I can't give you one simple answer. Words don't do justice to ordinary life, and they fail even harder when the life you're trying to describe is beyond ordinary. That said, I've tried in this book to give you a sense of the down-hill-uphill reality of life after paralysis.

Like all stories, it's only part of the story.

But if you want to know what it's like to be in my shoes now, I could start by telling you that I've owned my shoes for five years and they've never touched the ground. Thinking about that is enough to make me wonder—for the millionth time—about how things might have been different had January 16, 2013 been only a snow day off from school.

That might sound like I still struggle with negativity, but I've learned to be honest about the importance of both positive and negative thinking. There is tremendous power in positivity, but I think there's equal value in reflecting on the dark side of experience. Negative thinking is a map of my fears, worries, and doubts. Positive thinking is the path I draw on that map to find my way forward. There's a tension in that push-pull that has made me the person I am today, someone who finds motivation regardless of their fears.

Not that it's easy. My mind still wanders at night to good places and bad places before I fall asleep. And when I'm sleeping, I often dream of walking, running, or—best of all—playing sports. I feel the ball in my hands and the wind on my legs. I'm back in a time when I was free to roam around without feeling out of place. And then I wake up and sit with my able-bodied dreams, both figuratively and literally. I have to make a choice about not just what I need to do and want to do each day, but how I'm going to feel about the life I live. In other words, a positive attitude isn't just something you have; it's something you make.

No matter how motivated I am, though, I know that I don't do myself any favors if I fake how I'm feeling. There's a fine line between motivation and blind optimism. I don't always make the right choices, and like everybody else I still deal with indecision and doubt. But I learn from experience and move forward.

As I lay here in the early morning waiting for help to get out of bed, my mind is busy. On a typical day, I'll think about my plan: how I'll roll over to put my clothes on and remember to take my medication; how I'll be helped up to a position where I can scoot myself out of bed and over to the cushion of my chair; how I'll roll into my van and drive myself to work. Like everyone else, my day is filled with both chaos and the mundane, and I wouldn't want it any other way. I'm living an ordinary life, if under extraordinary circumstances.

But today is not an ordinary day.

I hear the creak of the back door. It's my father, and it's 5:16 in the morning. He strides into my room holding a coffee cup and flips on the light by the window next to my bed.

"Good morning!" he says, as if he thinks I want to have a conversation. As I pull the blanket from over my face to let in the light, I see him standing beside me with his "It's game day!" look on his face. It's a face I've seen quite a bit over the years, and despite my overpowering desire to pull the blanket back over my head, it makes me feel good.

He asks me if I'm nervous.

"A little bit," I say. But this wasn't a "Do you really want to do this?" question, but merely a check-in on my mental state before we get moving.

Feel the fear, but do it anyway.

"Let's go," he says, and I don't disagree. He pulls the sheets back and assists me with range-of-motion stretches for my legs. A few ups and downs, lefts and rights, and we're good to go. I take my meds before my dad helps me with the abdominal binder and hits the button to tilt my bed up. From a seated position I rock forward and use that momentum to shimmy slowly across the bed and onto my chair. I pull the joystick control down and flip the chair on.

It's still dark out.

I drive out of my bedroom and up to the glass door where I look out into the backyard. I don't know what I'm looking for, other than a distraction. My dad calls me back into my room to put on the clothes that I'll need for the day. Two long sleeves, long johns, a sweatshirt, and sweatpants: I'm ready for a morning that's still in the twenties. New England in mid-October isn't tropical.

While I eat a couple of breakfast sandwiches my dad moves through the apartment gathering everything we need to bring. I sit and blankly stare at the black TV, and I think about the past six months and wonder if I had really done enough training and preparation.

I signed up to ride a hand-cycle for the full length of the Baystate Marathon, and today is race day.

It's nice to feel the butterflies again. I haven't been in a position to compete for anything in nearly seven years. Some of the memories come back to me—bus rides to state playoffs and slow chairlifts to the top of the park—but this feels very different than my football games and snowboard competitions. I'm more excited than nervous. I need to get into it right away—the anticipation is eating away at me. I want to enter the zone again, to be that athlete for whom time disappears when the competition begins.

My bag is packed and it's time to drive the twenty minutes to downtown Lowell, where the race starts and finishes. I wheel outside into the crisp air, and it's cold. Really cold. I shake my head. 26.2 miles is a good distance to drive, much less ride a bike. And to run it? I imagine all the people who will be out there on the streets in shorts and T-shirts and think, *The hell with that.*

I wheel into the van and pull up to the driver's position while my dad pushes the bike up the ramp behind me, throws my backpack onto the back seat, closes the door, and climbs into the passenger seat. My bike is not what you might expect—it's actually one wheel and a chain with a hand crank that I secure to my manual wheelchair to create a three wheeled hand-cycle. It isn't designed for off-roading, but it's a cool, innovative technology that I had put to the test over the summer.

The sun peeks through the trees as I back out of my driveway and take off down the road. Dad and I are quiet, not because there's a lack of things to say but when I fall into the zone there's really no getting out of it. My dad knows that and limits his conversation to a couple check-ins along the way.

"You feeling good?"

A quick glance at the look on my face tells him all he needs to know.

I look over at Dad, and I flash on our second High Fives ski trip up to Sugarbush, in 2016. Being on the slopes again was just as amazing as the first time, but what made the trip really special was being part of an injury-prevention High Fives documentary called *BASICS—Five Critical Mistakes*. It's divided into sections called Speed, Shooting in the Dark, Dropping Your Guard, Know Your Line, and Ego vs. Intuition. My section was Dropping Your Guard, which makes sense. I knew the feature I built was sloppy, but I went ahead anyway. I hope that the documentary, like this book, keeps at least one kid safe and out of a chair.

They interviewed me about how the accident happened, and they talked to Dad about how hard it was for him as a parent.

"You walk into a triage room," he said, "and your son's lying on a table, wondering what's going on. A surgeon comes out, and he tells you that Jack's got a spinal cord injury and that the only way to resolve the problem at this point is with surgery. And then you find out that there's some paralysis involved. You're *hoping* that spinal shock is going to wear off after a few days, that he's going to start regaining some function . . ."—Dad took a breath—". . . and while he's there, it will all just start to . . ."—another pause—". . . come back." At that point he choked up. "I need a minute. I need a minute," he said.

He looked down and waited.

He talked about how my life changed. "He was a stud athlete. Captain of the football team, he's on the lacrosse team, he's just ready, you know, to . . .

"He's going to come back a different kid. But he came back the same kid, just in a different situation." Dad meant this as a compliment, I know, because he's saying that I came back a fighter even though the fight got a hell of a lot tougher.

In fact, now everything has kind of flipped on its head. Dad says that I'm teaching *him* about mental toughness. The flip side, though, is that he often reminds me that I don't show much emotion, and he's right. But this injury brought a lot of mental baggage, and being tough and stoic is one of my survival strategies.

About a mile down the road, I pull up to a red light at an intersection. I push the hand control brake with my left hand and look across the intersection at Old Stonehill Road as it curves up and out of sight. Just beyond the curve is a blue house on a hill with a shed at the top of a slope in the side yard. Several big bushes separate the yard from the quiet street. Though it's been seven years, I can still visualize the trip up that snowy street in my '99 Explorer to see Paul walking down from his house with his snowboard. That's one of several images from that day I will remember forever.

Now, Eric's house is for sale. Things evolve. Landmarks change their meaning. Life goes on.

The light is still red. Time enough for me to flash on that day and all the days that have come and gone since. I think about the people I've met and the work I've done and the decisions I've made, all of which has made me who I am today.

For me to say I could have imagined this day on the morning of January 16, 2013, would be ridiculous. But to say I could have anticipated it during my time in Atlanta or right after I got home would be equally ridiculous. It makes me realize, again, how the little things build and build into the story of one's life. You can only see so far ahead on the path you're traveling.

The light turns green as I try to make sense of where I've come from and who I might be down the road.

I turn left and think about all the training I did on these roads to get ready for the marathon. Cranking out mile after mile on Tyngsboro's country roads was exhausting, but it felt good to get stronger month by month. Neighbors and other supporters were always showing support by honking their horns as they drove by, which was nice, but to be honest it usually scared the shit out of me because I was in the zone and didn't know if the honking was friendly or a warning that I was about to be hit.

Which seems like a metaphor for life, right? You don't know what's coming until it hits you. Most of it is fine and good, the ordinary noise and motion of everyday life, but there's always that risk that something unseen will send you hurtling off your path.

I turn left onto the ramp for Route 3 heading south to Lowell. We're actually driving parallel to the race route now, which runs north up alongside the Merrimack River to Tyngsboro before crossing over the river and heading south.

On the highway I have time to think. A lot has changed in the years since the events of the book. I'm driving, I earned a business degree from UMass-Lowell, I have a job selling accessible vans at a dealership, and I'm a coach for Tyngsboro football. I've continued to move forward and manage all the little things in life too. I set goals and make progress. Looking back on these seven years, I'm proud of what I accomplished, and I'm sure that the next seven years will bring new challenges and new stories of overcoming them.

But much has stayed the same too. I still struggle with low blood pressure and low body temperature. I still use the cuff for my toothbrush and deal with spasticity every day. I still feel anxious if I'm stuck in one spot for too long, and despite all the long hours working out, I've probably only regained about 15 percent of the function in my triceps. I still have no neurological recovery in my lower body.

Every day I'm reminded somehow of the accident and its aftermath, and I still have all the post-accident messages of support on my phone. I still catch myself thinking: *What would I be doing right now if I hadn't broken my neck? What if I could have played college football? What if I was able to walk again?*

It's still incredibly hard not to be able to vent my emotion with my body—to run hard and burn off anger or sadness or confusion—especially when I realize again how difficult this has been for my family.

I still don't think that "everything happens for a reason," and I still think of God and religion as companions on my journey rather than a crutch to lean on. I don't pray to change my circumstances, because I still believe that regardless of who you are or what you do, things will happen that bring you joy, and things will happen that bring you pain. I look to find some order in the chaos and some good within the bad. I still wear a cross, but it's more about that kind of philosophy than a symbol of prayer and hope.

I still answer the same questions from people I meet: "Will you recover?" and "Will you walk again?" and "Can you feel this?" Others ask how my head is, whether I think I have the mental strength to keep my shit together. As old as it gets, I've always been open to these questions mainly because it keeps people talking to me. The worst thing to say to me is nothing at all. Don't be the person who is afraid to talk to someone in a wheelchair. They're the most interesting people I know, so say hi and give them a smile. It does wonders for self-esteem.

I still try to remember that everyone is struggling with their own story. Everyone has his or her own mental, emotional, or physical issues. I may not see the battle they're fighting, but it's on me to respect them for who they are and take the bad with the good.

I still haven't found someone to spend my life with, which isn't a surprise. I'm still young, of course, but being in a chair makes it hard to meet someone new. I think the hardest part is for a stranger to get past the first-glance concerns they might have about my injury. If they don't already know the story behind the chair—my story—then they probably won't try to get to know me.

At the moment, though, I'm about to mingle with thousands of people.

As we pull into the main entrance of the Tsongas Center in Lowell, we see runners and supporters arriving from all over. I steer through the crowds walking on the road and pull into the designated accessible area where I can park and unload my gear. As my dad grabs my stuff I wheel out of the van and into the parking lot where I see Ms. Craig and her mom. I'm not surprised to see her, because Ms. Craig was the one who convinced me earlier in the spring to do this race. It's great to see her, but it's also twenty-nine degrees Fahrenheit and I wonder to myself what the hell she got me into.

She and her mom are actually planning to do the mighty Boston Marathon soon. She hasn't stopped pushing me either. She's always asking me about what I'm doing next and how she can help. She sends me stuff on adaptive adventures, like a video of a guy on an adaptive mountain bike, with the question, "How can YOU do this?"

My dad scoops me up from my power chair and sets me into the manual. I push myself up to the front wheel portion of the bike and we secure it to make one three-wheeled machine. I wrap my wrists to add security for the hand crank that I'm otherwise not able to grip. A face mask to prevent wind burn and a helmet are the finishing touches.

Oh, and my tracking bib, which we realized a few minutes ago was sitting on my desk at home. Shit.

It's clear this happens often because a race volunteer is able to print another one for me. My dad isn't satisfied, though. He asks the volunteer if he can write on the bib. "It's something we had printed on the original," he says. "I have to write it. It means a lot."

"Okay?" she said, confused.

Dad writes Don't Be Lazy and slaps the bib on me right as Kim arrives to join him in seeing me off. I slowly pedal away from them toward the starting line. They wish me luck, as they have many times before.

I have fifteen minutes until the start, which will happen at 7:55 a.m., five minutes before the 1,200 or so runners. I'm thinking a thousand people breathing down my neck will be pretty motivating. There are seven other participants at the line with me, a few on hand-cycles and the rest as two-person teams like Ms. Craig and her mom. I sit by myself a few feet from the archway we'll pass through to start the timing. Sam and Mom come by to wish me a good race. I say, "Thanks," but not much else. I focus on the stretch of road ahead of me and pretend that it isn't below freezing. They understand and leave me sitting here.

The Little Things

I sit also with my disability. I cannot ignore it. It's hard for me to look at anything I'm doing and not think about how it would be different without paralysis. This five-minute head start is one more reminder of my difference in a constant flow of reminders every hour of every day. My response to all of it is resilience. After everything I've been through, the highest priority in my value hierarchy is to persevere. I can't control life, but I can control how I respond to its chaos and challenges. I do that not by cushioning the world to avoid risk but by using what I've learned when times were toughest.

That said, while there are days when I feel excited about the future, there are days when I ache to go back in time and begin again at age seventeen on the morning of January 16. Or any time at age seventeen. I don't want to erase my life as it actually happened, and I don't want to take a time machine back to childhood to make sure I never learn how to snowboard. I want a vacation from my disability. Just a day off, a day to walk about as I please, would be amazing. But no matter where I go in the world, the injury follows me. For all 26.2 miles of this marathon it will follow me.

I'd like to go back to a simpler time when I didn't have to wonder how to navigate an inaccessible world. Right when my friends and I were on the cusp of adulthood my life blew up. We all transitioned, but my transition was different. Life got real all at once and never stopped. No more days of minimal responsibility, no more mindless play. Imagine your life without any playing. For a lot of people that becomes their uncomfortable definition of adult life. For me, it was an early and lonely and permanent reality.

Well, permanent so far, at least. Since day one of my recovery, I've been keeping an eye on medical research being done to fix or treat SCI-related paralysis. The best-known treatment is stem cell therapy, in which stem cells derived from the patient are injected into the spinal column to encourage neural growth. It's been part of ongoing research around the world since before my accident, but until recently stem cell treatments weren't legal in the United States. I decided against it because I figured that if the US wasn't doing it, then it wasn't ready for prime time. Also, my family and I would have had to travel to someplace like Switzerland for an expensive treatment that has had mixed results. And, at this point, being several years past injury might hurt my chances at recovery, though I'm hopeful that better solutions will come along soon.

In 2014 a new treatment option—epidural stimulation—at the University of Louisville in Kentucky received a lot of media coverage because some research participants were able to walk again (with lots of assistance). An electronic device is implanted in the patient and attached to the spine in order to help reactivate whatever intact nerves still remain. Ideally this allows the brain to communicate a little with the paralyzed part of the body. The patients regain some voluntary movement, but not at a pre-injury level. What's amazing is that it's been effective even for people ten years post-injury. I know several people who are down in Louisville now receiving treatment. I haven't gone because it's hard for me to be one of the first participants in a trial. I want to know something works and won't cause more problems than it fixes. So far, like with stem cell treatments, none of the participants have regained enough function to get rid of their wheelchairs entirely. And though the trial is free, we'd have to live in Kentucky for at least a year without any income.

More recently, I've been in touch with a researcher at a company that has developed a serum that allows neurons to regenerate by canceling out inhibitors that prevent neuron growth. The researchers are doing clinical trials at various places around the country, and I've been talking to doctors at Spaulding Rehabilitation Hospital in Boston to see if it can happen there. If it does, then I may have a good chance of participating, since they're looking for cervical injuries that are at least a year old. It's a relatively simple procedure—not very invasive, just a spinal injection—that has had significant results in early tests. It's a Phase 2 trial, which means they already know it's safe enough to use on a larger group of participants.

It's hard to know what risks I should take when it comes to new treatments. If I'm too cautious, I might spend much of my life in a wheelchair merely because I was scared to try something. But there's no quick fix for a spinal cord. They call this experimental research for a reason. Experiments fail, and I don't want to end up with big debts or bigger medical issues because my body didn't like something that got injected into it. That said, I'll do everything I can to be ready, body and mind, for the right opportunity when it comes my way.

So I'm at the starting line in Lowell thinking about the past and the future at the same time. The road stretches out ahead and behind me. I am where I am with no end in sight to the work I have to do and the decisions I'll have to make.

I think it's natural that I still feel like two people—Jack before the injury and Jack after the injury—in the same body. I haven't forgotten the sense of freedom I once had even as I fully embrace who I am now. My eyes are open, and I'm not blind to reality. I'm very much here in this very real world, and though things don't always make sense, I do my best to deal with obstacles that nobody should have to deal with. There are days where simply getting up is a chore. When I feel like I've been sucked into an inescapable wormhole.

And that's a normal feeling. Life is hard. For all of us.

There are times, though, when you can put that shit in the background and set yourself up to rewrite the story of your limitations. To create a goal that you will stop at nothing to achieve. To reach a moment where your vision and preparation intersect, and you know no matter how it turns out that you worked so damn hard that you've become better than you thought you could. As an athlete, there's a lot to be said about creating those moments when the vision tunnels and the nervousness and doubts fade.

We owe it to ourselves to try to turn the traumas that haunt us into a story we can tell. And we honor our lives by deciding that the worst things that happen to us are not the most important parts of our story. There's love and family and the fundamental miracle of being alive.

I sit with my hands in my pockets and my breath coming out in clouds through the material of my mask. I am really here at the start, and for the next few hours I'll be alone, meeting the greatest athletic challenge of my post-accident life.

It's much more than a competition. I don't give a shit about winning. A medal means nothing. The sense of accomplishment, though, is what I want so badly.

And I want a vacation from the default mantra of the wheelchair-bound: I wish I could. Well, now I don't have to wish, because I'm doing it. And I get to share it with my family and a few close friends. No one else knows I'm doing this.

The race is seconds away and the PA announcer asks if we're ready. I look at him and then straight ahead. I slip my hands into the handles and take a deep breath.

"Go!"

And I go.

THE END

ACKNOWLEDGMENTS

First, to my family—the love has been true and consistent, and the support has never wavered.

I also owe a great deal to my friends with whom I've built strong bonds over the course of my entire life and who stood by me through tough times. Thanks also go to the town of Tyngsboro, which looked after one of their own; to the organizations and foundations that chose to support me during an incredibly difficult time; and to the members of the Jack Trottier Open Committee, who donate their time.

To Jason, who co-authored this complete rewrite of my original manuscript, I thank you for your patience and guidance through an unfamiliar world. Your creativity throughout the project allowed me to tell the story in the best way possible, and your gentle persuasion let me feel comfortable in doing so.